To

Mark

from

Crunt Margaret,
God Bless you—

Ralph's lastest book—

Thomas A. Easton
Ralph W. Conant

USING
Consultants

A Consumer's
Guide for
Managers

Probus Publishing Company
118 North Clinton
Chicago, Illinois 60606

This publication is designed to provide accurate and authoritative
information in regard to the subject matter covered. It is sold
with the understanding that the publisher is not engaged in
rendering legal, accounting, or other professional service.
If legal advice or other expert assistance is required, the
services of a competent professional person should be sought.

FROM A DECLARATION OF PRINCIPLES JOINTLY ADOPTED BY A
COMMITTEE OF THE AMERICAN BAR ASSOCIATION AND A
COMMITTEE OF PUBLISHERS.

Library of Congress Cataloging in Publication Data

Easton, Thomas A.
    Using consultants.

    Bibliography: p.
    Includes index.
    1. Business consultants.   I. Conant, Ralph
Wendell, 1926–   II. Title.
HD69.C6E24   1985   658.4'6   84-25404

ISBN 0-917253-03-5
Library of Congress Catalog Card No. 84-25404

Printed in the United States of America

1 2 3 4 5 6 7 8 9 0

Preface

We have written this book for one major reason: To provide guidance to the business community in selecting consultants. Businesses often call upon consultants for assistance in every area of their operations, and there are a great many consultants of every kind. Any business person who feels the need for help needs answers to these questions:

What are consultants?

What are their special qualities?

What good can they do a business?

What do they cost?

Are they worth the cost?

How can a business find the right consultant?

How can a business use consultants to best effect?

Unfortunately, the answers were not easy to find before this book was written. The answers were buried in the pages of business magazines and journals. There are not many up-to-date books that address them at all.

Our purpose is to answer these questions one at a time and in detail. We hope our work will help business people unravel the complexity of the consulting industry, find appropriate help, and use it to enhance their success in America's fiercely competitive marketplace.

If we have succeeded, it is because many people have made their research and wisdom available to us, both personally and through their publications. Among those who have given their personal help are Howard L. Shenson, J. Michael Jeffers, Wayne R. McGuirt, Mark A. Greenberg, and David A. Lee. Our shortcomings are our own.

Thomas A. Easton
Ralph W. Conant

Contents

1

Should You Consider a Consultant?

Success requires the honesty to recognize one's limitations.

In business, success requires more than just a salable product or service. It requires the knowledge of how to sell that product or service. It requires the ability to organize a company and its operations, find adequate financing, control costs and inventory, hire effective workers, and manage and motivate people. But no single person can be expert in every aspect of business. Many managers commit costly errors out of ignorance or lack of experience. They needn't. Ignorance can be eliminated by learning what you need to know, lack of experience by seeking help from experienced people.

To be successful in business, you don't have to know *all* there is to know about business, but you have to know *when* and *where* to seek help, and *how* to use it. That is what this book is about.

3

In business, one important source of help is the consultant, the expert in one or more phases of your business. The purpose of this book is to explain what kinds of consultants exist, where to find them, what good they can do, what they should cost, and how to get your money's worth.

In this introductory chapter we ask the question, "When and under what circumstances should you consider hiring a consultant?" and in answering this question, we explain how to decide to use a consultant. We hope our answers to this and later questions will make success more likely for you.

Some consultants are specialists; others are generalists. Some consultants specialize in setting up new businesses. Others deal with personnel, executive compensation, management information systems, marketing, organization, strategic planning, computers, production, advertising, capitalization, accounting, stock offerings, human dynamics, and so on. Many consultants belong to professional associations that attract consultants with similar specialties. We list many of these associations in Chapter 8 as an aid to helping you find the right expert.

The categories of consulting expertise that are available to businesses are discussed in detail in a later chapter. It is enough here to point out that the kind of consultant you call upon depends on the needs of your business. The start-up period calls for a start-up specialist. What kind of start-up specialist you need depends upon your prior knowledge and experience, the nature of your business, the intensity of the competition, and your problems of financing and production.

At a later stage, the choice of a consultant depends upon the nature of the specific problems you encounter. A word of caution: It is not unusual for a firm to be in serious trouble before anyone in the firm has identified the difficulty.

We discuss the diagnosis of problems later in this chapter and also in other chapters in the book. By way of preliminary comment, the business person should be aware that apparent problems in one area can be due to real problems in another area. In an extreme example, bankruptcy can be due to low or poor advertising or poor sales performance. Poor sales performance might in turn be due to an understaffed, poorly paid, or inadequately trained sales department. An experienced consultant can figure out the root cause and recommend ways to solve the problem.

As we shall emphasize throughout the book, the identification and defining of problems can be among the most important services a consultant provides to a business client.

THE IMPORTANCE OF FLEXIBILITY

One of the basic reasons for business failure is sheer bullheadedness. Bullheaded business executives are absolutely sure they know how to run their businesses. Their attitude toward anyone who might help is "HANDS OFF!" Some bullheaded executives seem to prefer to fail on their own rather than to thrive with help.

There are bullheaded people who are successful. They are the ones who know their businesses inside and out or have little or no competition. Such people and situations are rare. The modern business environment is one of intense competition. It allows little time for muddling through, and there is always someone watching for weakness.

Luck is seldom a big factor in business success. What we call luck is usually the result of a well-prepared person recognizing and taking advantage of a new opportunity, or creating one. This is true of the salesperson who assiduously calls upon company after company and—not by accident—is there the day the customer decides to buy. It is true for the entrepreneur who meets a venture capitalist on the plane and has in an attaché case the home-built prototype for a new diddley-whocker.

Successful business people recognize their limits. They are prepared to seek help when they truly need it, and to pay for it. Those who do not seek or accept help when they need it are asking for trouble.

In this chapter we are focusing on the considerations that should go into a decision to hire a consultant. One of those factors is how you anticipate using the results of the consultant's work once it is done. A common complaint of consultants is the client who engages them to analyze a problem and to prepare recommendations, and then ignores the advice. Such clients increase the odds against their success. The odds improve for business people who hire good consultants and use their advice.

As a business person contemplating a substantial expenditure on a consultant, you should bear in mind that using advice requires being open to change and being ready to listen to other views. It also requires the capacity and willingness to take a new path.

Effective use of advice also requires a healthy skepticism, the ability to ask, "Does an existing practice work?" If so, then leave it alone. If it ain't broke, don't fix it. But if it doesn't work, admit it and be ready to consider alternatives. Call in a consultant to spell out the alternatives. Try them and question them all until you find one that proves out.

CONSULTANTS AS SPECIAL RESOURCES

You need a consultant if you need a technical expert to fix something in your business. Consultants are "fix-it" specialists, but they can also be useful to managers who recognize their own ignorance. A good consultant has the up-to-date, in-depth knowledge needed to design effective marketing plans or competitive compensation plans. There are consultants who have the skills and contacts to find executives. There are others who can get whatever information you need. As you will learn later, there are consultants for just about any problem that comes up in your business.

Consultants are supplemental resources, walking reference books, and they can be extra hired help. Yes, extra hired help. Sometimes a business lacks the personnel to do a job and does not want to hire a full-time permanent employee for what may be a temporary need. Consultants can be put on the payroll for a specific period of time to do a specific job. They bring to temporary assignments their expertise and ability to perform studies, write reports, and design products—whatever you need on a temporary basis.

FOCUSING ON THE PROBLEM

Consultants do not like to tackle false problems. Suppose that a business person hires a consultant to improve sales by improving the training of the sales force. The consultant works for months designing a training program and for additional months actually training sales people. But what if the real problem was an inappropriate reward system? The consultant will fail to improve sales, and both the consultant and the client will be unhappy.

We have in mind an actual case where the cause of poor sales lay in motivation. The sales people were paid by commission, which had worked well during the initial marketing period when penetration was still low. As penetration expanded, sizable commissions became hard to come by and the sales people grew demoralized. The answer was not training but supplementary salaries.

How can the business person avoid such errors in diagnosis? The answer is that the business person who is considering hiring a consultant should always present a diagnosis to a consultant as a suggestion, never as a firm, unalterable assignment. This approach leaves the consultant free to find and focus on the real problem.

We should add that an experienced consultant in such a situation would not have accepted the assignment as presented by the client. An experienced consultant always reexamines any problem described by the client and if necessary redefines it. The competent consultant never takes the word of the client for the nature of a problem in the business any more than a competent physician accepts the diagnosis of the patient. In fact, some consultants specialize in diagnosing problems and recommending the consultants who are needed to work out solutions.

We can see a good example of how consultants redefine problems as their clients perceive them in what one of us did when asked to help a public library system establish services for a city's legal, business, and government communities. His first step was to ask a crucial question: "Do the local professional communities have any interest in using the public library system?" He then performed a formal survey among the local professionals and found that the answer was a very clear, "No!" All three sectors said they had customary sources of research and information that satisfied their needs. In other words, he found that there was no market for the service his client wished to offer. His next step was to recommend that the library system invite

7

the local professionals to participate in planning a library service they *would* be interested in using.

One of the best times to consider hiring a consultant is when you are having trouble defining a problem clearly enough to see the solution. There are, of course, good reasons why you may be unable to define problems accurately. One reason may be lack of time. You are constantly busy with decisions to be made, conflicts to be ironed out, emergencies to be attended. You may never have the time to reflect upon the underlying problems that may be keeping your business from realizing maximum profits.

A second obstacle to accurate problem definition may be lack of analytical talent. Many executives are very good at making decisions and managing people but not good at gathering and synthesizing information. Some executives are not good at breaking a problem into its components to study the interrelationships of the pieces. Others may lack the experience to distinguish potential causes or to tell which of several contributing causes is the most important.

A third obstacle is bias. Like everyone else, you have blind spots, vested interests, and prejudices. Having put the time, effort, and money into doing things in one way, you may be unwilling to consider a different way of doing things. Some people, having been trained in one approach, may be unable or unwilling to recognize the value in alternatives. Coming from one school (or industry or country), they may be unwilling to admit that worthy talent may come from other sources.

The talent obstacle may be overcome by calling upon a consultant. The time obstacle may be overcome if you are willing to take the time for serious reflection. The bias obstacle requires nothing less than a disciplined change of thinking.

To beat bias requires the habit of questioning. We usually associate this mode of thinking with the constantly skeptical academic scientist. It may seem tiresome to the average person, but the habit of questioning is a very effective approach to solving difficult problems. The hallmark of the skeptical thinker is a reluctance to take anything for granted, a driving urge to ask the question, "Is this really the problem?" and a willingness to consider alternatives, asking, "But what if we did it *this* way?"

When one goes to a physician with a complaint, the physician

8

sees a "presenting complaint." This is the symptom; it may or may not be what the physician will have to treat. The physician will consider the symptom and then probe, test, and question to find the cause behind the symptom. Once the diagnosis is established, the treatment can be prescribed. Perhaps the treatment will involve a specialist.

Where there is a problem in business, there is always a "presenting complaint." The consultant, like the physician, probes beyond the symptom to find the true cause of the problem. The consultant is helped when you as the client have also done some analytical probing. Moreover, you are ahead if you have acquired the discipline and ability to analyze the trouble to the point where you can decide whether outside help is needed. If you have acquired the discipline and ability to analyze the trouble, you will find working with a good consultant can be a very satisfying mutual experience.

Always bear in mind this common-sense rule of survival: When in doubt, look for expert help. You need help if you feel confused and panicky, for these are sure signs that you are in over your head. *Not* going for help when you face trouble you cannot handle is self-destructive.

Most consultants believe that management should attempt to define its problems before calling in a consultant. If management is successful in the analysis, a solution can usually be worked out without any outside assistance. If the trouble is identified but a solution is not evident, management is at least in a position to select the right consultant and outline a clear assignment.

Executives who define problems successfully use very much the same methods as consultants. Faced with a symptom such as poor sales, the executive asks, "Why?"

- Is new competition cutting into the market? If so, why?
- Does the competition have a superior product?
- Does the competition have better marketing methods?
- Has the market shifted?
- Has the competition lowered or kept down its prices?
- Has the company lost efficiency in production or run its costs up with high inventories?

9

The executive also considers the competence and motivation of the sales force.

- Does the problem lie with personnel, training, or compensation?
- Does it lie with middle-management leadership styles (rude, dictatorial, laissez-faire)?
- Does the problem lie in marketing, advertising, billing, or customer service?

Any of these areas could be the root of the problem. The point is to ask every reasonable question and to examine systematically every available clue.

Where do you find the information to answer these questions? In the same place a consultant will look:

- In financial, sales, and other internal reports that contain company data usually available from a well-designed management information system;
- In interviews with production, sales, and administrative employees;
- In interviews with customers; and
- From observation of the interpersonal styles of managers.

Precise, accurate answers to these questions can help you locate the faulty element in your corporate machinery. But fixing that element is often less important than achieving a particular end result. For instance, you can stop customer complaints either by improving quality control or by lowering prices. Your choice of solutions depends on many factors, including not only cost and benefit, but possibly urgency and perhaps even political and regulatory constraints.

If you decide to take the first steps toward identifying the source of problems in your firm, it is important to start with a list of the symptoms that alerted you to trouble. Exhibit 1-1 is a list of typical symptoms that point to trouble in business organizations. Your list may or may not resemble ours.

Does your company have any of the symptoms that appear in Exhibit 1-1? If so, ask yourself why. Some of your symptoms may be explained by others on your list. Try to link that symptom

Exhibit 1–1   First Signs of Trouble

Poor sales	Too many rush orders
Episodic sales	Sporadic production
Poor profits	Lack of new products
Poor cash flow	High absenteeism
Slow decision-making	Poor safety record
Customer complaints	Unfilled positions
Slow order filling	High inventory
Excess overtime	Low inventory
Too little information	Too much information

to another one on the list. You should consider, for example, whether customer complaints are due to slow order fulfillment, and whether the latter is due to low inventory. Poor cash flow, on the other hand, could be due to high inventory, poor sales, poor profits (in spite of good sales), slow billing, or cost overruns.

Slow decision-making is a common complaint. It may be due to either too little or too much information about what is going on in the company—or, say, to an excess of rush orders. Smoothing out the work flow may help by giving people the time to provide necessary information. Filling vacant positions may also help—unless that problem is itself due to slow decision-making. An improved management information system (MIS) can cut down on excess information, or ensure adequate information. Improving the MIS may require purchase or replacement of a computer, of a software package, or of a programmer.

The solution to a problem such as slow decision-making may ease other problems. The solution could open the way to expansion in time to take advantage of new markets or new economic conditions— or to retrench in time to avoid a disaster.

THE DIAGNOSIS AND AFTER

Tracking a problem to its ultimate cause can seem difficult, or even impossible. But an accurate diagnosis of the problem will

11

always lead to a workable solution. Philip H. Shay (1981) describes the consultant's approach to diagnosis and solution in four stages: research, analysis, solution, and installation.

The research stage begins with planning the work by defining its purpose and scope. What is the work intended to accomplish? How much ground should the study cover? What is out of bounds? On the basis of the research, the consultant organizes the work, estimates the fact-finding time, and determines the product. At this point, the consultant can actually begin to collect facts to use both in studying the problem and in seeking a solution.

The analytical stage begins with defining the problem. Once the problem is defined, the consultant can use collected facts to determine the cause or causes and the possible solutions.

In the solution phase, the consultant and the client select one of the possible solutions and design the blueprint for implementation. In the installation phase, either the consultant or the client's managers implement the blueprint. Often the consultant is retained to supervise the implementation. The consultant-client relationship may thus continue long past the initial diagnostic stages.

DO YOU NEED A CONSULTANT?

How do you know when you have found the cause of a problem? It is not always possible to know for sure. You can identify symptoms and track problems from cause to cause until you can go no further. Sometimes the process of tracking takes you in circles. Once you have reached a point where further tracking is unproductive, it is time to stop and think through what you have found. A consultant would do the same. Similarly, when writers researching a new topic reach a point where new references begin to repeat previous ones, they know it is time to stop the research and commence writing.

The difference between you and a consultant in this situation is that a consultant, with more experience and greater objectivity, may be in a better position to evaluate the relative importance of the observed causes. Also the consultant may be less likely to overlook crucial evidence. A consultant who has seen your problem in other settings may be in a position to interpret the available facts with greater accuracy and thus arrive more promptly at a workable solution.

If you have been careful and thorough and if the company has the personnel and funds to implement a solution, then it may be unnecessary to hire a consultant. If, on the other hand, you lack the confidence in your analysis or the resources to implement your solution, or if your solution did not work, then you must call in a consultant. Having done the analysis, you are probably very well prepared to choose the right consultant and to provide that consultant with a clear assignment. Furthermore, you will be in a good position to understand and implement the solution recommended by the consultant.

Once you have concluded that you need a consultant, you should be as clear as possible about the assignment. Spell out in writing what you expect the consultant to do; what problem you want the consultant to address; and what approach you think should be taken. Most consultants will ask for your definition of the problem and for your suggested approach. In many cases the consultant will then proceed to redefine the problem and develop an approach that may be different from the one you suggested.

What the consultant wanted from you in asking for your definition of the problem was an insight from your point of view into the nature of the problem. What you have to say about the problem at the problem definition stage will give the consultant important clues. The consultant's redefinition of the problem does not reflect on your judgment; it tells you that the consultant brings in-depth, objective experience to your problem. It also tells you that the consultant is giving your problem serious original thinking that will probably result in a solution tailored to your company's needs.

When the consultant proposes a satisfactory approach, get that proposal *in writing.* The resulting document will serve as a standard against which to appraise the consultant's performance as well as a basis from which to negotiate changes should the need arise. We have more to say about negotiations with the consultant in Chapter 7.

If this statement seems only common sense consider the

finding by Peterson and Kerin (1980) that marketing research buyers and suppliers thought it important to define needs and put proposals and other communications in writing. Many business people fail to follow this basic principle. Too often in dealing with consultants, otherwise hard-headed business people put too much trust in good intentions and faultless memories. We all know the kind of trouble to which that fundamental error can lead.

2

When Are Consultants Necessary?

In Chapter 1, we observed that a consultant is necessary whenever you have a serious problem in your business that you have not been able to solve. Your inability to find a solution may be due to any of the following:

- You have not had the time to analyze the cause.
- You do not have the skills or tools to study the problem.
- You know or believe you know the cause, but you need help working out a solution.
- You know the cause and the solution, but you need expert help in the implementation.
- You have the capability within your firm to solve the problem, but an outside consultant could do the job in a few days or weeks without disrupting the work of your regular staff.

These are also some of the most common reasons a business person decides to hire a consultant. There is usually some risk involved. Once you have decided to hire a consultant, there is no way of being absolutely certain of the wisdom of the move until the job is completed and the results show up in the operations of the company. Only when the consultant's efforts lead to developments that would have been otherwise impossible can one say for sure that the consultant was essential.

IS YOUR STAFF AN OPTION?

It may be possible to do without outside help, but perhaps only by compromise and persistence. Compromise means taking time you do not believe you have to pursue the study and analysis of the problem or assigning a competent staff member to do the job. Persistence means grappling with a situation until you or a staff member comes up with a plausible solution.

You may find the time, the imagination, and the resources to master a problem that you doubted you or your firm had the capability to solve. Employees often have unsuspected abilities not tapped by their regular duties. The production worker who serves in spare time on a volunteer fire squad or civil emergency team could be the right person to set up a plant safety program. The file clerk who writes science fiction nights and weekends may be the person to produce a company newsletter to provide opportunities for individual recognition and improving morale.

Discovering unused talent in an organization is a routine function of a management consultant. So is developing new talents among appropriate employees, either by setting up training programs or by recommending that management sponsor outside educational programs. For instance, paying for courses in industrial safety or traffic management could well result in cost effective improvements in worker safety or in the improved efficiency of a shipping department.

Sometimes a manager actually feels embarrassed when a consultant turns up talent that the manager missed. However, the consultant can succeed because the manager often fails to think beyond official job descriptions. With just a little creative thinking, a manager can find or encourage the development of the talent to fit particular needs or to solve seemingly difficult problems, and then the consultant may not be required.

It is easy to justify hiring a consultant in hindsight. But you are also justified in hiring a consultant whenever the value of needed improvements can be projected to outweigh the cost of the consultant. When such projections are uncertain, then potential intangible benefits should be considered.

You may see problems that threaten present and future operations even though you may be unable to make precise projections of the harmful effects you suspect may occur. Such problems may involve morale, worker productivity, image, or customer relations. The decision to hire a consultant in such cases may turn not so much on hard evidence of potential damage to operations as on your experience in recognizing warning signals. The role of the consultant may be limited to minor adjustments that head off serious problems or the consultant may need to formulate a plan for major changes.

Even in cases where the company has the internal talent and resources to tackle the problem, it may not be possible to assign staff people to problem solving. And only large companies with a constant flow of problem situations can justify employing a full-time staff consultant or releasing a valuable executive from other responsibilities.

Some companies feel that in the interest of economy they must rely on their executives to work on problems as they arise in addition to their routine management tasks. The drawback to this all-too-common arrangement is that staff executives almost never have the time to study a serious problem thoroughly enough to come up with the optimum solution. A conscientious executive will find a solution, but not necessarily the optimal one.

No matter how dedicated and hard-working, the full-time executive is usually too absorbed in day-to-day responsibilities to spare the hours, days, or weeks required to address larger problems with the necessary thought and attention. The executive may also lack the up-to-date expertise to solve the problem.

The unavailability of company talent to solve a problem often shows up after management has identified a problem, tried to solve it, and failed. Management then finds it reasonable to call in a consultant.

Thus a consultant is necessary when you cannot spare the staff time and resources to do the job. Usually a consultant can justify his or her presence on the job in terms of cost saving. A consultant may also bring to the job broader experience and more specialized knowledge and skills than members of your own staff. The consultant brings two other crucially important elements: objectivity and impartiality. The experienced consultant will serve as a catalyst and leader to get the job done expeditiously. The best consultants bring fresh ideas to every project they handle.

THE NEED FOR RESOURCES

The most common reason for engaging a consultant is the need for more resources than the company itself can bring to bear on a problem. Frankenhuis (1977) observed that a consultant supplies imaginative solutions for the present and specialized advice for the future. The latter covers most cases, for many corporate problems involve planning for future growth, profits, investments, products, marketing, site development, and so forth. However, although such problems are the ones consultants most often work on, the value of the results can be open to serious question. This is because a consultant's effectiveness depends upon the client's ability to define his or her needs, understand the consultant's recommendations, and use them.

The greatest value of any consultant is breadth and variety of experience in the client company's problem area. Given the time, company executives—or their successors—could probably come up with solutions to most problems that arise. The advantage of experienced consultants is that they have probably solved similar problems for other companies. While busy executives try to divert valuable time and energy into problem solving, an outside expert is in a position to zero in on the problem quickly and efficiently.

Jerome Fuchs (1975) lists several reasons for calling in consultants. The first is when a board of directors exercises its function as an overseer of management performance and says "Hey! You need help!"

The second is when the company recognizes that it does not have the internal staff with the needed expertise to perform a critical assignment. As an example, it has become common for corporations to "farm out" the environmental impact statements that federal and state governments require when plant or facility expansion is likely to have major physical or social consequences. These impact statements can involve elaborate and sometimes very difficult methods that sometimes require unusual expertise to complete. A few years ago, the Commonwealth Edison Corporation of Chicago called upon one of us to do the social and economic impact study of a proposed nuclear generation station in western Illinois. The project involved projecting the impacts of about 2,000 construction workers on a rural area over varying periods of up to seven years. The major technical difficulty in the research was how to interview 2,000 to 2,500 workers at three similar sites in various stages of construction. Approximately 90 to 95 percent of the workers at each site had to be interviewed without any work stoppage or disturbance. This formidable task was accomplished by careful interview design, step-by-step negotiation simultaneously with union officials and company managers, and skillful execution of a very precise interview plan. The company hired the consulting team to do this job because it had neither the time nor the expertise to carry it out itself.

Fuchs' third—and more substantive—reason is the need for help with budgets, sales forecasts, cost projections, and other elements of a company's profit plan. This assignment requires careful analysis of trends in sales, costs, market characteristics, and industry performance.

Managers who lack experience or training in developing comprehensive profit plans need the expertise of the outside consultant until they acquire the personal or staff competence to do the job. Managers who are competent in profit planning but find their energy and that of their staff absorbed by other responsibilities also need outside expertise.

A good consultant is often able to come up with a better plan than even the most competent management can do on its own.

Once again, the reason is that the consultant is likely to bring greater objectivity and broader experience to the assignment than the company managers.

In making this point, Fuchs gives the example of a major aluminum company whose marketing consultants projected no long-term profitability for one product line and greater than expected profitability for several other lines. As a result, the company phased out the first product line and expanded the others.

Fuchs' fourth reason is one we mentioned earlier: Companies often need specialized skills for brief periods. They need a product designed or tested, pilferage stopped, packaging developed, a market analyzed, a report written, or a construction site evaluated. Lacking suitable people on their staffs, they seek part-time help—consultants.

Fuchs' fifth reason for using consultants is to help in long-term strategic planning. Long-term planning plays an important role in short-term profit plans and guides overall company policy in five- to ten-year time spans for the benefit of chief executive officers and boards of directors. A company's long-range plan helps middle managers and other employees to understand board and executive actions that relate to long-term considerations that may seem in conflict with near-term conditions.

The objectivity, perspective, and experience of a first-rate management consultant are especially valuable in assignments that call for long-range planning and the formulation of multi-year plans. Management consultants who regularly work in the area of long-range planning can bring to bear their knowledge of trends in the client's industry, including regional, national, and global market conditions. They can also factor into long-range company planning any social, political, and economic trends that might affect the future prospects of the company and decisions on long-term commitments.

Consultants who work on long-range industrial planning are aware of how other companies in the industry are adjusting their plans to future market conditions. They routinely apply this knowledge to their client's planning efforts without violating the confidences of other clients and colleagues.

Good strategic planning involves a great variety of specialized knowledge. Managers ordinarily are not trained in all of the relevant areas of economics, market and product research, financial management, diversification, mergers, and so forth. On the other hand, consultants who specialize in long-range planning have the requisite training and experience in these areas, and when necessary they supplement their personal expertise with the specialized knowledge of colleagues and associates.

Continuity is very important in long-range planning. An expensive plan can be wasted in a change of management where the new team is unaware or unappreciative of the plan's value to policy-level decisions. In the circumstance of a new management team, the board of directors should consider calling in the consultant who wrote the company plan for the purpose of briefing the new managers on the plan. Should changes be required in the plan to take into account new policies, the adjustments can be made as part of the board's continuous planning process.

Planning consultants know better than anyone that a plan is useful only if it is administered as a flexible instrument that can be adapted to new conditions by policy makers who understand planning as a continuous process.

During a hiatus between management teams, the company's planning consultant may be the best choice for an interim manager. Such a measure can provide beneficial continuity during the period of transition.

When there is a major change in company product or a new market adaptation, the consultant can play a crucial role in planning and coordinating the changes required by the new strategy. Fuchs cites the example of a yacht company that shifted from wooden to fiberglass boats. The change required economic forecasts and changes in production techniques and facilities, as well as a new marketing arrangement involving franchises. Since no one in the company had the experience to plan the transition, a consultant was hired for the job; his duties included retraining and reorienting employees.

A sixth reason for hiring a consultant is to deal with problems that arise out of sudden or rapid change, such as an unexpected deterioration in profitability due to management weaknesses or incompetence, overexpansion, a restrictive labor contract, a precipitous drop in sales, or increased imports. External factors that might cause a company to call in a consultant might be

23

unforseen changes in the industry or the economy, the health of the market, new government policies affecting regulation of the market, new government policies affecting regulation of the industry, or energy prices and supplies. In any of these cases, a consultant may be essential to analyze the severity of the problem and to recommend ameliorative action.

The critical need is for fast, decisive, appropriate action. The necessary consultants may be technical specialists, marketers, or public or labor relations experts. In addition, financial consultants may be essential to provide a full understanding of the problem's impact on the company's profitability. Solutions may involve developing new product lines, finding alternative energy supplies or reducing energy usage, or getting out of one phase of the industry and into another (for example, getting out of manufacturing and into importing).

As this book is being prepared for publication, the Federal Trade Commission has decided that the American shoe industry needs no relief through tariff protection from the imports that have captured 74 percent of the domestic shoe market. One shoe manufacturer in Maine has decided to become an importer of Brazilian shoes. He will continue the manufacturing operation for the time being, but he is prepared to abandon that activity in the future if import competition dictates.

THE NEED FOR VALIDATORS

Consultants fill a company's need for a resource that is lacking, but they also fill other critical needs. Albert S. Dexter and Bernard J. Schwab (1975) join other writers in observing that some business people in search of a consultant do not really want independent, objective expertise.

What they want instead is validation, an expert to confirm a decision they have already made. They may want this confirmation to protect themselves against anticipated criticism or merely to ease lingering doubts they may harbor. They may need a credible outsider to take the heat if something goes wrong.

Reputable consultants are willing to be used as validators, but they do not like to be used as scapegoats. Nor do they like to be called in as status symbols. Consultants who are willing to be used as status symbols or scapegoats may not have strong enough reputations to be valuable even in these questionable roles.

The validation function is a legitimate one. A business executive or entrepreneur faced with an unfamiliar or difficult problem or breaking new ground understandably may lack confidence to forge ahead unaided, even when plans are laid and basic decisions made. They need someone they consider to be an expert to say, "You are on the right track. Go with it."

The role of validator is, however, one that can be unjustifiably restrictive. The consultant likes the client who says, "We are looking at these possibilities. Help us to evaluate them and add any others that you believe we should be considering." Most consultants do not like to be asked, "Are we right?" Nor do they like to be told "Make us look good." Consultants can make a far greater contribution when "Make us look good" becomes "Help us improve."

Public relations specialists do concentrate on making their clients "look good," but management consultants see such an assignment as a perversion of their usefulness. Even public relations consultants—the most reputable of them—often advise clients on ways to improve products and services so that the image they create comes as close as possible to matching the reality.

Validation is not legitimate when it involves sneaky, roundabout political ploys. Consider the company president who, because of a personal grudge, wants to get rid of a vice-president. The president decides on a reorganization plan that will leave the vice-president out of a job. The president hires a management consultant to put an "objective" seal of approval on the plan.

The consultant who accepts the job without looking into the reasons becomes, in the parlance of the profession, "a hired gun." The legitimate course for the president to follow would be to hire a process consultant to work on the problem of the bad relations with the vice-president. The work of the consultant could result in the eventual resignation of the vice-president if the incompatibility cannot be resolved. Or it could result in a resolution of the problems between the two executives.

25

Validation is not legitimate when it is used as a weapon in company politics. Two executives may have differing views of what should be done in some area where their responsibilities conflict or overlap. If they cannot or will not agree on a common approach, one may try the ploy of calling in a consultant to endorse the favored approach or to discredit the colleague's approach. Either way, the consultant is being asked to take sides in a situation where an objective evaluation is required.

The proper role of the consultant in such situations is that of evaluation and arbitration. The appropriate consulting specialty here is conflict resolution. Failing a successful resolution between the two adversaries, the consultant should be asked by a superior to recommend replacement of one or both adversaries.

Many arbitration consultants are members of the American Arbitration Association, a non-profit organization with a membership of 60,000 professionals, many of whom are psychologists. AAA arbitrators often enter the picture when partners find themselves unable to get along. The arbitrators thus become corporate "marriage counselors."

Robert A. Mamis (1984) describes several cases where consultants were essential in this role. In one case, two men set up a chemical company after leaving their jobs as a sales representative and a financial officer. Ten years later, they were refusing to speak to each other, locking each other out of their offices and selling off company assets behind each other's backs. Their personalities clashed, their priorities differed, and each one wanted to be boss. They wound up in receivership, which might have been avoided if an appropriate consultant had been called in at an early stage in the conflict.

Mamis tells us that such cases are not rare. They are common enough to give impetus to a new area of consulting called business-dispute resolution. Some attorneys thrive on taking unresolved cases into the courts, a time-consuming and wasteful means of settling such disputes.

Personality conflicts and competition for power are only two of the many factors behind disputes in the business world. Serious conflicts can also arise when partners begin as close friends—perhaps as college chums—and grow in different directions. Disputes can arise when one partner's life changes, as in the aftermath of a divorce, marriage, or family death.

Disputes can spring from the interference of family members or from the dynamics of parent-child relations or from sibling rivalries. These factors can be similar to those that lead marriages into divorce, and so it seems reasonable in such circumstances for one or both parties to a potentially damaging dispute to consider calling in a consultant who specializes in working on interpersonal relations.

COMPANY DIFFERENCES

The problems that call for consultants vary from one company to another. The big companies seek help in strategic planning for diverse product lines, decentralization, management information systems, market research, new product testing, anti-trust litigation, management development, compensation studies, and acquisitions. Their structures and their problems are complex, and they need consultants with varied expertise and personnel and with large capabilities in support services. The big companies thus tend to rely on the larger consulting firms rather than the smaller, local ones.

The larger consulting firms nurture their relations with the big corporations by frequenting the same country clubs and civic and business associations. Also, the big, prestigious companies seek what they consider to be the best and most prestigious consultants. The reason is that chief executive officers can defend and justify recommendations made by Arthur D. Little or McKinsey where questions might arise over recommendations by a little-known firm from Albuquerque.

The executives of the big companies are more likely to think of themselves as more experienced and better educated than those of small companies. As a consequence, they are more likely to emphasize the validation function of consultants. They are more likely to want confirmation of their own ideas or recommendations they can compare with alternatives they have already considered. The staff experts of the big corporations,

27

including internal consultants, are working on the same problems, and they can be just as talented as the outside consultants. In addition, big companies are often unwilling to let consultants handle implementation of recommendations.

In privately held companies with few stockholders, the pattern is different. Management decisions may have personal and emotional rather than financial bases. The managers and board members may be in their positions more because of ties of family and friendship than because of competence. Management does not readily think of calling in consultants to resolve organizational disputes and difficulties.

When consultants are brought in, they are usually ones who also have personal ties to people in the company. The efforts of a consultant in this kind of situation can seldom depart from diagnosis and explicit, resource-oriented advice. They ordinarily are not in a position to consider solutions that might involve replacing incompetents.

A variant of the privately held company is the family-owned business, whose managers and employees may be related by blood or marriage. Family businesses share the traits of privately held companies, but they suffer added complications from sometimes painful entanglements of family relationships.

Sibling rivalries, for example, can interfere with efficient management, with hiring, firing, promotions, and succession. So can the demands of family members whose involvement in the business is limited by their need for income; it is not uncommon for income demands to block needed expansion or capital improvement.

In the case of family-owned companies, the consultant's task is often to convince family members that professional management should prevail over family politics. The consultant can convey the message that the long-run good of the company is in the long-run interest of the family and that the long-run good can be best served by improved family communications and relations. The consultant can also focus on arranging for the business to survive family deaths and battles over wills.

Nonprofit organizations also deserve to be included in any discussion of business needs for consultants. Their operating budgets and salaries are usually low in comparison to profit-making businesses and so they find it difficult to attract highly qualified managers. It is mainly for this reason that they need periodic consulting help to improve their operations. For the same reason many of them need grant and fund-raising advice. Cost cutting can be an important issue with nonprofit organizations, as can the sensitive matter of motivating underpaid personnel. Consultants can help in both areas.

Different types of industries require different types of consulting help. Manufacturing needs help with problems of capital, inventory, product development, and marketing. Service businesses, being more labor intensive, also need help with marketing, but their most vexing problems usually involve labor issues and human relations, compensation, training, and motivation.

Chemical companies and businesses operating in health care and medicine are particularly vulnerable to suits over issues of malpractice or environmental contamination. Utilities, railroads, mines, and pharmaceutical companies are subject to heavy governmental regulation. In each case, the conditions of the industry largely dictate the problems that require the help of consultants.

Economics also plays a role in determining an industry's need for consultants. Fading industries, such as steelmaking, are forced to cut costs and move into other, more profitable enterprises in order to preserve their stockholders' interests. Growing industries, such as electronics, computers, and biotechnology, must invest heavily in research and development as a strategy for success. The new "high tech" industries must market their products aggressively and take enormous risks to reap the rewards of the pioneer. Extraction industries such as metals, paper, and oil have learned to expand vertically, using the large profits from finished products to support the extraction of raw materials from the earth and forest.

Industries also differ in the technical problems they face. These problems can be so unique and important that they define the industry. Consider the aerospace, chemical, extraction, energy, publishing, transportation, and many other industries. Each requires consultants with particular kinds of expertise.

Aerospace engineers, for example, need to be able to design and build machines that fly. Publishers need to know how to produce books from rough manuscripts.

THE UNIVERSALS

Despite all the differences among companies and among the tasks and competencies expected of consultants, there remain some common needs shared by most companies. These common needs are reflected in certain skills that are required of all consultants. Companies need consultants who are sympathetic to their special needs. The needs may be for validation, advice, information, cost savings, or profit boosts. It is these needs that make the consultants necessary in the first place, and so it is the satisfaction of these needs that defines the consultant's value to them.

When you need a consultant, you should try to find one who has a reputation for putting the interests of the client first. You should avoid those you feel may try to impose preconceived notions of what your company needs or prepackaged solutions from other jobs.

Joseph P. Kahn (1984) quotes Jerry Reilly, comptroller of the Laminaire Corporation, as saying, "I'd had quite a bit of experience with management consultants, and most of it was poor. These guys came in and told you what you should be doing, without delving into what people in the company were actually trying to do. In all my years at bigger companies, I never saw a consultant's plan implemented in its entirety. But I did see an awful lot of bruised feelings."

Kahn's aim in his commentary was to laud a "new breed" of management consultant, exemplified by Henry Ekstein, head of Management Resources, Inc., in Teaneck, New Jersey. Ekstein is an "interactive consultant" who draws solutions to problems from his client's own people. He works closely with the people who will be most affected by any changes, involves them in the problem analysis, and ensures that they share credit for the solution. Thus he eliminates the sense of threat many outside consultants arouse. In the process he induces a commitment to

30

make changes work. He observes, "The better the consultant's advice, the greater the resistance to it."

Ekstein has had notable success with smaller companies, thanks to his spread-the-credit approach. Harold Kaye, executive vice president and general manager of Remington Aluminum, says Ekstein's greatest asset is "mind expansion." He explains, "Henry starts talking out ideas and then takes me further and in more directions with each idea than I could ever get myself."

Ekstein says that he finds smaller companies interesting because their people have many dormant ideas that bear on company problems. He considers it his task to awaken these ideas and, in addition to solving problems, to change how management thinks and thus to improve managers' ability to solve their own problems.

Ekstein's approach is fundamental to sound, productive consulting. It is not a new approach. Two decades ago, one of us was asked by the Greater Hartford Chamber of Commerce to help business and civic leaders in Hartford to organize a three-day conference on metropolitan problems. The stated objective was to persuade Hartford area leaders of the necessity and desirability of reorganizing the dozen or so towns and cities comprising the Greater Hartford region into a single metropolitan municipality. Instead of accepting the assignment as presented, the consultant persuaded Chamber leaders of the need to establish a process of leadership education on the issues involved in a proposed governmental reorganization as a preliminary step to a conference. The educational process commenced as a collaborative effort between a team of experts in local government and politics and a steering committee made up of the heads of twenty Hartford- based companies. The experts, under the direction of the steering committee, ran field investigations of various aspects of the metropolitan government proposal. On the basis of the studies (which took place over a period of six months), the steering committee formulated a series of reports and drew up some recommendations, one of which was to call an area-wide conference of citizens to consider the steering committee's findings. The conference was named "Town Meeting for Tomorrow." The conference attracted 650 area citizens representing every interest group the steering committee (by then greatly expanded) could find. The conference was organized as a series of round-table discussion groups, each focussed on an aspect of the steering committee's work. The consulting team members were available as resource people to interpret or explain the background information from their field studies. After two days of discussions, the discussion groups turned in consensus reports to "writing committees" of the steering committee. The writing committees collaborated on a final report of the conference which the conference, sitting as a town meeting, was asked to approve. The conclusions were practical, realistic commentaries on governmental conditions in the region and included recommendations for intergovernmental cooperation and legislative action. The following year, the state legislature set up a temporary commission to establish enabling legislation for local intergovernmental cooperation. About the same time, the Chamber of Commerce initiated a broad-based civic improvement project that became the nationally recognized "Hartford Process." In the entire Town Meeting for Tomorrow project, the consultant was never in a position of initiating recommendations or providing solutions. The outcome was wholly the work of the citizen participants with no more than process and organizational guidance from the consultant and the team of experts.

The interactive approach to problem solving, as illustrated by the Hartford example and currently by Ekstein's work, is being used by more and more consultants who have background and training in the psychology of creativity and interpersonal relations. Consultants who leave behind lasting beneficial changes in the way their clients think about problems are worth far more than the technicians who merely fix problems.

3

What Kinds of Consultants Are Out There?

Have you decided that you have a problem that requires a solution? Is the solution unavailable within your firm? If the answer to both these questions is yes, then you should seek outside help. Usually, this means seeking the services of a consultant.

Going to a consultant is not the admission of failure that some inexperienced executives believe it is. Seeking help means that you are committed to success, that you want to take advantage of the state of the art in building your business and meeting its needs. The state of the art in your business is what a competent consultant can provide.

The growing awareness of this simple fact is why the consulting industry has been able to grow so rapidly in recent years. In 1984, consultants earned more than $3 million in revenues nationwide. Three quarters of these revenues were from businesses of all types and sizes. The rest came from government and nonprofit institutions.

The major hazard in using consultants is in choosing the *wrong* consultant. An error means wasted time and money. It also means that a critical problem may go unsolved. An unsolved problem could lead to poor performance and lost profits, even to bankruptcy.

Avoiding the hazard of the wrong consultant requires an understanding of what kinds of consultants are available and what they can and cannot do. We consider what consultants can do in Chapter 4. In this chapter, we look at the great variety of consultants to be found in the field, their qualifications, and the ethical codes to which they subscribe.

WHAT IS A CONSULTANT?

Consultants are people who offer specialized knowledge and skills, such as technicians, engineers, financial experts, and technical writers. As specialists for hire, consultants offer services or expertise not available within your business or not needed on the regular company payroll.

Technical people who work as consultants include:

aerospace engineers	geophysicists
architects	graphics artists
biologists	hydrologists
chemical engineers	meteorologists
chemists	mathematicians
civil engineers	metallurgists
climatologists	political scientists
economists	psychologists
educators	roboticists
electronics engineers	sociologists
environmental scientists	soil chemists
ethicists	statisticians
geneticists	technical writers
geologists	and editors

Some technical consultants work as consultants full time; others work as consultants part time. Some of the latter are retired professionals or university faculty members. Some of the jobs they undertake include testing chemicals and drugs for toxicity, evaluating sites for new buildings, projecting trends, designing buildings or production lines, devising new products, preparing proposals and reports, and assessing and training personnel. The list is endless, yet part-time and full-time technical consultants are only a small portion of the consulting industry.

Most consultants are management consultants. This portion of the consulting industry includes over 6,000 firms of two or more employees and 40,000 to 50,000 full-time individual consultants. There may be over 70,000 management consultants if we count part-timers. Management consultants are people who are qualified by training and experience to help businesses and other organizations analyze management problems, recommend solutions and, when necessary, aid in implementing the solutions.

The Institute of Management Consultants lists the following "common consulting specialties":

- Research and development
- Financial planning and control
- Human resources management and labor relations
- Manufacturing
- Compensation: wage and salary administration
- Incentive compensation, etc.
- Physical distribution
- Physical distribution
- Sales and marketing
- Administration
- Electronic data processing
- Organization planning and development
- Strategic planning and development

CONSULTING FIRMS

Every one of the "common consulting specialties" just listed can be found within the largest of the national "general management" consulting firms such as McKinsey & Company and Booz,

Allen & Hamilton. These firms and others in their class have offices in the nation's larger cities, as well as in countries around the world. They do most of their business with large companies.

A second major component of the consulting industry are the "Big 8" CPA firms, such as Arthur Andersen. Their principal business is accounting work, including audits. They also offer their clients help in financial analysis, computer systems, and information systems. Some of these firms concentrate their efforts in specific industries such as banking or manufacturing. Some of the large CPA firms have separate management consulting groups associated with them.

Other consulting firms may specialize by function, such as sales, administration, or financial, organization, or strategic planning, offering assistance based on broad experience with specific kinds of problems. Still others deal with all companies of a particular type: automobile manufacturers, metal fabricators, banks, garment makers, and so forth. Their assistance is based on broad experience within an industry. They have seen many kinds of problems and solutions, and they are expert at interpreting the forces in labor, markets, resources, and economics that affect companies.

Some consulting firms specialize in the public sector "industry"—federal, state, and municipal governments, schools, and planning and regulatory agencies. These firms have people who are experts in the legal, political, and economic constraints on public activities and take these constraints into account in recommending courses of action for officials. They formulate policy, draft legislation, draw up long-range planning documents, rewrite municipal charters and state constitutions, and organize conferences for citizen education. Some public sector consultants are former public officials; others are from university faculties.

"Think tank" firms like Arthur D. Little are staffed by university-quality consultants who specialize in problems requiring extensive research and innovation. Teams of experts direct the research and base some of their work on original projections of trends into the future. Some of the experts associated with these firms are professors who are based in nearby universities.

The "think tank" firms are an invaluable resource to firms

that need to know how various hard-to-calculate factors—from politics to climate—will affect their business one or two decades hence. They have on tap specialists ranging from technical experts to management consultants, many of whom are members of university faculties.

The fees of the large consulting firms are usually high in comparison to consulting fees overall (see Chapter 5), but this fact should not deter smaller businesspeople from considering them. The "think tank" type of consulting firm could be of special value to businesses in new and rapidly developing industries where the stakes are high and the competition fierce. Any firm with a new product and good market potential should seek the most competent consulting assistance available, even if the price looks high.

Businesses with a new and promising product are well advised to seek top-quality consulting help *before* they think they need it. The "think tanks" are especially good at working with innovators in the early stages of their product and marketing development.

Many large consulting firms, including the "think tanks," seek the business of small organizations, and they usually take into consideration the size of the company in their bids and proposed budgets. The best of the big consulting firms, including the "think tanks," take the view that the problems of small companies are as important as the problems of large companies. Small companies can be charged proportionately less because in smaller operations there is less to study in coming up with a solution.

Many small businesses (see Exhibit 3-1 for definitions of "small" in business) prefer to work with small consulting firms. The lower fees of the small consulting firms (based on their lower overhead) are an attractive feature. For some businesses a smaller consulting firm may be more accessible than one of the larger ones, for there are hundreds of small firms serving local and regional areas.

An advantage of small consulting firms is their ability to offer intensive service on an "on call" or retainer basis. Small businesses find it easy to develop close, long-term relationships with small, nearby consulting firms. A further advantage is that the

Exhibit 3–1   Small Business Administration definitions of small businesses, as eligibility requirements for SBA loans (1981)

Industry	Definition
Manufacturing	Maximum number of employees may range from 250 to 1,000, depending on the industry in which the applicant is primarily engaged.
Wholesaling	Yearly sales must not be over $9.5–22 million, depending on the industry.
Services	Annual receipts not exceeding $2–8 million, depending on the industry.
Retailing	Annual sales or receipts not exceeding $2–7.5 million, depending on the industry.
General construction	Average annual receipts not exceeding $9.5 million for the three most recently completed fiscal years.
Special trade construction	Average annual receipts not exceeding $1 or $2 million for the three most recently completed fiscal years, depending on the industry.
Agriculture	Annual receipts not exceeding $1 million.

small consulting firm is unlikely to assign inexperienced persons to a job or to shift personnel in the midst of a project.

In contrast, large consulting firms sometimes lose people through resignations. On occasion they move their best people from small projects to larger, more exciting or lucrative ones, to the disadvantage of the more "ordinary" projects. Such shifts have a greater impact on smaller business clients than on large ones.

A disadvantage in working with small consulting firms is that they may lack the resources of larger firms. Big computers or graphic arts departments are examples. The more sophisticated small consulting firms can overcome this disadvantage through carefully planned subcontracting. No competent consulting firm large or small, will undertake a job that is beyond the resources available to it. An important task in selecting a consultant is to make certain the firm you choose can demonstrate that it has, or has access to, all the resources that are necessary to complete the assignment you have specified. As a safeguard, your attorney should draw up the consulting contract. We will have more to say about the dos and don'ts of selecting a consultant in Chapter 7.

The smallest consulting "firms" are the individual practitioners. Some of these practitioners are generalists. The most effective ones may be highly skilled specialists who typically work with a small number of clients. Some individual consultants are nationally recognized experts on particular kinds of problems. Some of the individual practitioners consult full time; others are university-based professors or retired professionals who work as consultants part time.

TYPES OF CONSULTANTS

There are clearly several types of consultants. Each type is suited to addressing specific kinds of problems, but they may also differ profoundly in their basic approaches to problems. When you go shopping for a consultant, you will find great differences among consultants, even among those who are in the same category. Learn these differences well, and bear them in mind when you get ready to make your choice.

The types we will discuss here are: diagnosticians, change-oriented consultants, specialists, the so-called "content" consultants, process consultants, and internal consultants (available only to the companies for whom they work).

Diagnosticians are often generalists who use broad education and experience to deal with many kinds of problems. They tend to restrict their efforts to studying a company, identifying problems, describing the problems in detail, and recommending solutions. The diagnosis can be enough for some business clients, but many clients need assistance in implementing the recommended solutions.

The follow-up to the diagnostician consultant is the *change-oriented consultant* whose expertise lies in implementing recommendations. Change-oriented consultants actually help clients

41

solve problems: they train employees, find new executives, set up computer and information systems, and so forth.

The *specialist consultant* is retained to carry out an assignment or to solve a specific problem which either the client or a diagnostician has identified. In hiring a specialist, it is important for the client to be clear about the exact nature of the assignment. The specialist should not be expected to "second guess" the appropriateness of an assignment or to offer unsolicited advice about company problems outside the area of the specialized assignment.

Content consultants have the knowledge necessary to develop and present a solution to a specific problem. The problem you present to the content consultant will be the problem for which you get a solution. Content consultants are not likely to include other, related problems in their reports.

Process consultants believe the client possesses all the necessary knowledge; they see their role as making the client aware of that knowledge. Process consultants ask questions to help the client define and refine the problem at hand and to see the solution. Psychologists and psychiatrists are process consultants; hence process consultants are usually trained in psychology. Their work is akin to psychotherapy, focussing on human interactions. They obtain their most effective results when, in fact, a company's problems lie in personality conflicts.

In considering the type of consultant that might best fit your needs, we advise avoiding those who peddle prepackaged solutions. Any of the types of consultants discussed in the preceding paragraphs might follow this dubious practice. Consultants who do offer prepackaged solutions usually defend them on grounds that they should work well because they were successfully used by other companies with similar problems.

It is our experience that the soundest results come from consultants who treat each client as a unique case and provide custom-tailored solutions. The custom-tailored solution takes more time and is therefore more expensive that the prepackaged solution, but the results are sure to be a better "fit." Further, the study necessary to tailor a solution to your particular needs may well turn up additional problems with the potential for future trouble.

It is true, of course, that the consultant who uses the custom-tailored approach is also adapting experience with previous clients to your situation.

A very different kind of consultant from any of those discussed above is the *internal consultant.* As we indicated, this consultant is not likely to be available. We describe the internal consultant here for the benefit of the reader who may be in a position to consider employing one in his or her company.

The internal consultant is a luxury ordinarily affordable only by large companies whose organizational complexity calls for continuous expert attention to management problems. In such cases, a full-time consultant (or staff of consultants) can save the company considerable time and money. A full-time legal staff is a parallel.

The internal consultant has the advantage of intimate familiarity with company problems and constant opportunities for beneficial change. The internal consultant is both a specialist whose expertise is one particular company and a generalist who must be a diagnostician as well as a skillful implementer of solutions.

Robert E. Kelley (1979) observes that internal consultants can provide more rapid responses to problems, are more accountable for their work, and are more cost effective than external consultants. They are especially useful as researchers, analysts, trouble shooters, advisers, critics, and screeners. Kelley also argues that internal consultants can serve as training grounds for future high-level managers. Outside consultants are preferable only when the company needs temporary help, an outside opinion, or specialized expertise that is not available internally.

The most important limitation of the internal consultant is a crucial and inevitable lack of objectivity. Kelley cautions that the internal consultant who tries to be honest and objective can get into the position of antagonizing superiors. The internal consultant may also lack the experience and insight that the independent consultant acquires from exposure to the problems of many different companies.

Some large companies, including Control Data Corporation, AT&T, and Polaroid, among others, have established their

43

internal consulting operations as profit centers. Their consultants sell their skills to other companies, as well as to the parent company. Their expertise is specialized, but it is enormously enriched by exposure to the problems of other clients. Thus, they may represent a uniquely qualified resource for other companies, both large and small, in related lines of business.

THE QUALIFICATIONS OF CONSULTANTS

Anyone can become a consultant. All that is necessary is a sign on the door, a business card, a letterhead, and a client or two. There are no authoritative requirements that legitimize the profession or give protection to inexperienced clients.

It is thus essential that any businessperson who is considering hiring a particular consultant pay careful attention to the consultant's background and reputation. Technical consultants should possesss at least a masters degree in their specialty; a doctorate is preferable. Management consultants should have a masters degree in business administration (MBA) from an accredited institution. Management consultants should show evidence of specialized study in areas of claimed expertise, such as finance, marketing, or planning. A degree is not an essential credential only when the consultant is well qualified by experience.

The consultant's knowledge should represent the state of the art in his or her specialty. The client should look for evidence that the prospective consultant has kept abreast of new developments in the field by participating in courses, seminars, institutes, and symposia. Some leading consultants keep up-to-date by advancing the state of the art themselves, frequently lecturing and writing.

The most successful consultants know how to probe deeply into a problem, where to look for causes, and how to understand them, and therefore how to devise precise, workable solutions. In addition, they know the language and culture of business and can quickly develop a productive rapport with their clients. Above all, they can communicate effectively in their reports and in training staff who are charged with carrying out solutions. They may well have gained many of their skills through long experience as consultants or by working within the industry of their specialty. Either way, they have great familiarity with the problems and possibilities of the field.

Most professions have established procedures and standards that certify their members as qualified in their field. There is no one organization that certifies consultants, and so there is no universal system of certification by which a businessperson in search of a consultant can short-cut the evaluation of a consultant's qualifications.

Groups such as the Professional and Technical Consultants Association require only a certain period of full-time consulting practice to qualify for membership. Thus a listing of membership in the credentials of a consultant is not necessarily reliable evidence of professional competence.

There are certification programs for some types of consultants. The Institute of Management Consultants and the Institute of Certified Professional Business Consultants are both recognized and respected in the field. The Institute of Management Consultants awards the title of Certified Management Consultant (CMC) to members who have at least five years of full-time consulting experience, at least one year of major project responsibility, six references of which three must be from recent clients, written summaries of five major assignments, including one in great detail, and a qualifying interview. The interview rates professional competence in areas of specialization, experience, understanding of the current state of the art, ability to communicate, and knowledge of and commitment to the Institute's Code of Professional Conduct. The Institute rates competence on the basis of practical experience as well as professional training.

Members of the Institute of Certified Professional Business Consultants may use the letters CPBC after their names. Qualification requires five years of assisting physicians, dentists, and other professionals with the management of their practices. The certified Professional Business Consultant must also subscribe to the Institute's Code of Ethics and Rules of Professional Conduct and pass a rigorous examination. The examination deals with management of medical and dental offices, fees, credit, debt

45

collection, ethics, and government regulations. A second part of the examination deals with financial management, group practices, retirement plans, estate planning, and taxes. The examination is intended to certify the technical competence of the consultant in this field.

Professional qualifications are as important in consulting as they are in any field, but of equal importance in consulting are the personal qualities of integrity, responsibility, intelligence, and creativity, and the ability to get along with all kinds of people.

Integrity is honesty in describing one's training and experience; commitment to producing useful results at a reasonable cost; and unwillingness to cut corners, pad bills, accept kickbacks, or misrepresent situations under investigation. Integrity should be evident in references from previous clients.

Responsibility means both promising no more than one can deliver and delivering no less than one promises. The responsible consultant makes accurate estimates of costs, stays within the contract budget, and meets deadlines. The consultant's firm has or has reliable access to the resources that are required to complete the assignment.

Consultants should also be intelligent, insightful, creative people able to analyze situations, see relationships among facts, and devise workable and, when appropriate, innovative solutions to the problems they confront. The most competent consultants demonstrate these qualities in publications that contribute to the state of the art in their fields.

The consultant must be able to get along with the client and with the client's associates and employees. A good personality match between consultant and client can help a difficult assignment go smoothly and efficiently, ensure acceptability of results, and leave the client satisfied with the consultant's performance. A bad match can make satisfactory results almost impossible to achieve.

Finally, the consultant should be an independent thinker, a good listener, an energtic team worker, and a person who inspires confidence that a solution is possible. Successful consultants are also reflective, self-aware people who have their own sense of worth. They need it, for they get surprisingly little gratitude from their clients.

46

THE CONSULTANT'S ETHICS

We reproduce the Code of Ethics and the Standards of Professional Practice of the Association of Management Consulting Firms (ACME) in the Appendix to this chapter. The Standards represent the aspirations and the ideals of ACME. The Code is intended as a binding guide to professional behavior and practice. ACME investigates complaints against members who are accused of violations and takes disciplinary steps to correct abuses.

The Code emphasizes the importance of independence, impartiality, objectivity, and confidentiality. It requires that members avoid conflicts of interest, reveal unavoidable conflicts, and stay out of fights between clients. ACME members seek assignments only on objective criteria, accept only jobs they believe they can do effectively, guarantee no specific results other than practical recommendations, and are committed to aid in implementation. They promise to work only with full information, to share their techniques, methods and principles for training purposes, and to charge reasonable but adequate fees.

The Standards promise continual improvement of competence, sharing of knowledge with clients, the public, and other consultants, and quality control. Consultants who abide by the Standards also refrain from "stealing" the employees of their clients and other consultants and from advertising their services in self-laudatory ways.

Other professional consultants have similar, but often less detailed, codes of ethics. The Professional and Technical Consultants Association includes items on equal opportunity, seeking and accepting honest criticism of work, and protecting public safety, health, and welfare. Members of the Association of Consulting Chemists and Chemical Engineers (ACC&CE) promise to "expose and oppose all quackery and fraud," to avoid illegal work and questionable enterprises, and to refuse to work for clients who have treated other consultants unfairly.

ACC&CE members also promise to resist efforts to reduce their fees once they have been set. They hold to the principle of "intellectual" property: Ideas, designs, inventions, and processes developed from client information belong to the client; those developed out of the consultant's own knowledge or creativity belong to the consultant.

The Code of the Institute of Certified Professional Business Consultants has relatively few items, but it does dictate professional conduct based upon "integrity and high moral purpose . . . in the best interest of clients." The Code also binds the Institute's members to dignified, judicious advertising, and it makes members accountable to the Institute's Board of Examiners.

Accountability is also provided for by the Institute of Management Consultants (IMC). Members pledge to abide by the Institute's Code of Professional Conduct, and members can be disciplined for failing to live up to the Code. The IMC's Code is similar to ACME's; it adds a prohibition against deliberately using the proprietary data, procedures, materials, or techniques, without permission, that other management consultants have developed but not released to the public domain.

The Association of Management Consultants has a brief Code of Professional Practice that covers most of the ground of the others. Unlike the others, it prohibits the use of contingency fees (see Chapter 5). The rationale is that such fees can compromise objectivity.

All the professional codes have the same purpose: to ensure that consultants behave with integrity, responsibility, and courtesy. Consultants who abide by the codes give their clients few reasons for legitimate complaints. They avoid situations which they are not equipped to handle, and their work is likely to be reliable.

Codes of ethics and standards of professional practice also provide moral support to consultants faced with clients who ask them to behave dishonestly or unprofessionally. The consultant is in a position to say to the client: "I do not do this and you will not find a reputable consultant who will." Thus, the codes of consultants provide support for their reputations as well as some measure of contract security.

Consultants who abide by the codes of their professional societies can usually be trusted, but this trust should not be taken for granted. Not all consultants belong to professional societies; not all professional consultant organizations have codes of professional conduct; and not all consultants always abide by the codes of their profession. You as a client should always address ethical issues when you interview a consultant. Standards of professional conduct should also be covered in the consultant's contract.

APPENDIX

Code of Ethics and Standards of Professional Practice of the Association of Management Consulting Firms (ACME, Inc.)*

PREAMBLE

Purposes of the Code of Ethics and Standards of Professional Practice

The Code of Ethics and Standards of Professional Practice signify voluntary assumption by members of the obligation of self-discipline above and beyond the requirements of the law. Their purpose is to let the public know that members intend to maintain a high level of ethics and public service, and to declare that—in return for the faith that the public places in them—the members accept the obligation to conduct their practice in a way that will be beneficial to the public. They give clients a basis for confidence that members will serve them in accordance with professional standards of competence, objectivity, and integrity.

The Code expresses in general terms the standards of professional conduct expected of management consulting firms in their relationships with prospective clients, clients, colleagues, members of allied professions, and the public. The Code of Ethics, unlike the Standards of Professional Practice, is mandatory in

*Reprinted by permission of The Association of Management Consulting Firms, Inc.

character. It serves as a basis for disciplinary action when the conduct of a member firm falls below the required standards as stated in the code. The Standards of Professional Practice are largely aspirational in character and represent objectives and standards of good practice to which members of the Association subscribe.

The Association enforces the Code of Ethics by receiving and investigating all complaints of violations and by taking disciplinary action against any member who is found to be guilty of Code violation.

The Professional Attitude

The reliance of managers of private and public institutions on the advice of management consultants imposes on the profession an obligation to maintain high standards of integrity and competence. To this end, members of the Association have basic responsibilities to place the interests of clients and prospective clients ahead of their own, maintain independence of thought and action, hold the affairs of their clients in strict confidence, strive continually to improve their professional skills, observe and advance professional standards of management consulting, uphold the honor and dignity of the profession, and maintain high standards of personal conduct. This Code has evolved out of the experience of members since the Association was incorporated in 1933. In recognition of the public interest and their obligation to the profession, members and the consultants on their staffs have agreed to comply with the following articles.

I–Code of Ethics

1. Basic Client Responsibilities

1.1 We will at all times place the interests of clients ahead of our own and serve them with integrity, competence, and independence.

We will assume an independent position with the client, making certain that our advice to clients is based on impartial consideration of all pertinent facts and responsible opinions.

1.2 We will guard as confidential all information concerning the affairs of clients that we gather during the course of professional engagements; and we will not take personal, financial, or other advantage of material or inside information coming to our attention as a result of our professional relationship with clients; nor will we provide the basis on which others might take such advantage. Observance of the ethical obligation of the management consulting firm to hold inviolate the confidence of its clients not only facilitates the full development of facts essential to effective solution of the problem but also encourages clients to seek needed help on sensitive problems.

1.3 We will serve two or more competing clients, or clients in any known adversary relationship, on sensitive problems only with their knowledge. Under certain circumstances we recognize that the adversary relationship may be such that service to both clients is inappropriate and we would have to discontinue our relationship with one.

1.4 We will inform clients of any relationships, circumstances, or interests that might influence our judgment or the objectivity of our services.

2. Client Arrangements

2.1 We will present our qualifications for serving a client solely in terms of our competence, experience, and standing, and we will not guarantee any specific result, such as amount of cost reduction or profit increase.

2.2 We will accept only those engagements we are qualified to undertake and which we believe will provide real benefits to clients. We will assign personnel qualified by knowledge, experience, and character to give effective service in analyzing and solving the particular problem or problems involved. We will carry out each engagement under the direction of a principal of the firm who is responsible for its successful completion.

2.3 We will not accept an engagement of such limited scope that we cannot serve the client effectively.

2.4 We will, before accepting an engagement, confer with the client or prospective client in sufficient detail and gather sufficient facts to gain an adequate understanding of the problem, the scope of study needed to solve it, and the possible benefits that may accrue to the client. The preliminary exploration will be conducted confidentially on terms and conditions agreed upon by the member and the prospective client.

2.5 We will, except for those cases where special client relationships make it unnecessary, make certain that the client receives a written proposal that outlines the objectives, scope, and, where possible, the estimated fee or fee basis for the proposed service or engagement. We will discuss with the client any important changes in the nature, scope, timing, or other aspects of the engagement and obtain the client's agreement to such changes before taking action on them—and, unless the circumstances make it unnecessary, we will confirm these changes in writing.

2.6 We will perform each engagement on an individualized basis and develop recommendations designed specifically to meet the particular requirements of the client situation. Our objective in each client engagement is to develop solutions that are realistic and practical and that can be implemented promptly and economically. Our professional staffs are prepared to assist, to whatever extent desired, with the implementation of approved recommendations.

2.7 We will not serve a client under terms or conditions that might impair our objectivity, independence, or integrity; and we will reserve the right to withdraw if conditions beyond our control develop to interfere with the successful conduct of the engagement.

2.8   We will acquaint client personnel with the principles, methods, and techniques applied, so that the improvements suggested or installed may be properly managed and continued after completion of the engagement.

2.9   We will maintain continuity of understanding and knowledge of clients' problems and the work that has been done to solve them by maintaining appropriate files of reports submitted to clients. These are protected against unauthorized access and supported by files of working papers, consultants' log-books, and similar recorded data.

2.10 We will not accept an engagement for a client while another management consulting firm is serving that client unless we are assured that any conflict between the two engagements is recognized by, and has the consent of, the client. We will not endeavor to displace another management consulting firm or individual consultant once we have knowledge that the client has made a commitment to the other consultant, unless we are assured that the client is aware of any conflict between the two commitments.

2.11 We will review the work of another management consulting firm or individual consultant for the same client, only with the knowledge of such consultant, unless such consultant's work which is subject to review has been finished or terminated. However, even though the other consultant's work has been finished or terminated, it is a matter of common courtesy to let the consulting firm or individual know that the work is being reviewed, provided that the client consents to such disclosures.

3. Client Fees

3.1   We will charge reasonable fees which are commensurate with the nature of services performed and the responsibility assumed. An excessive charge abuses the professional relationship and discourages the public from utilizing the services of management consultants. On the other hand, adequate compensation is necessary in order to enable the management consulting firm to serve clients effectively and to preserve the integrity and independence of the profession. Determination of the reasonableness of a fee requires consideration of many factors, including the nature of the services performed; the time required; the consulting firm's experience, ability, and reputation; the degree of responsibility assumed; and the benefits that accrue to the client. Wherever feasible, we will agree with the client in advance on the fee or fee basis.

3.2 We will neither accept nor pay fees or commissions to others for client referrals, or enter into any arrangement for franchising our practice to others; provided, however, that two or more consulting firms or individuals may agree as to sharing of any fee or commission on a basis reasonably commensurate with the relative values of the services performed for the client. Nor will we accept fees, commissions, or other valuable consideration from individuals or organizations for recommending equipment, supplies, or services in the course of our service to clients.

II—Standards of Professional Practice

In order to promote highest quality of performance in the practice of management consulting, ACME has developed the following standards of good practice for the guidance of the profession. Member firms subscribe to these practices because they make for equitable and satisfactory client relationships and contribute to success in management consulting.

1. We will strive continually to advance and protect the standards of the management consulting profession. We will strive continually to improve our knowledge, skills, and techniques, and will make available to our clients the benefits of our professional attainments.

2.   We recognize our responsibilities to the public interest and to our profession to contribute to the development and understanding of better ways to manage the various formal institutions in our society. By reason of education, experience, and broad contact with management problems in a variety of institutions, management consultants are especially qualified to recognize opportunities for improving managerial and operating processes; and they have an obligation to share their knowledge with managers and their colleagues in the profession.

3.   We recognize our responsibility to the profession to share with our colleagues the methods and techniques we utilize in serving clients. But we will not knowingly, without their permission, use proprietary data, procedures, materials, or techniques that other management consultants have developed but not released for public use.

4.   We will not make offers of employment to consultants on the staffs of other consulting firms without first informing them. We will not engage in wholesale or mass recruiting of consultants from other consulting firms. If we are approached by consultants of other consulting firms regarding employment in our firm or in that of a client, we will handle each situation in a way that will be fair to the consultant, the firm, and the client.

5.   We will not solicit employees of clients for employment by us or by others, except with the consent of the client. If we are approached by employees of clients regarding employment in our firm or in that of another client, we will make certain that we have our clients' consent before entering into any negotiations with employees.

6. We will continually evaluate the quality of the work done by our staff to insure, insofar as is possible, that all of our engagements are conducted in a competent manner.

7. We will endeavor to provide opportunity for the professional development of those who enter the profession, by assisting them to acquire a full understanding of the functions, duties, and responsibilities of management consultants, and to keep up with significant advances in their areas of practice.

8. We will administer the internal and external affairs of our firm in the best interest of the profession at all times.

9. We will not advertise our services in self-laudatory language or in any other manner derogatory to the dignity of the profession.

10. We will respect the professional reputation and practice of other management consultants. This does not remove the moral obligation to expose unethical conduct of fellow members of the profession to the proper authorities.

11. We will strive to broaden public understanding and enhance public regard and confidence in the management consulting profession, so that management consultants can perform their proper function in society effectively. We will conduct ourselves so as to reflect credit on the profession and to inspire the confidence, respect, and trust of clients and the public. In the course of our practice, we will strive to maintain a wholly professional attitude toward those we serve, toward those who assist us in our practice, toward our fellow consultants, toward the members of other professions, and the practitioners of allied arts and sciences.

Adopted February 1, 1972; amended September 19, 1978; amended November 2, 1981; amended January 25, 1982

Questions about interpretations or Code violations should be sent to:

President, ACME, Inc.
230 Park Avenue
New York, New York 10169
212/697-9693

4

What Can
A Good
Consultant Do?

When is a consultant truly necessary? It is a fact that careful, thoughtful analysis of a problem often reveals the solution. Thus, if you have succeeded in defining the problem, you may well have also found the solution. In this happy circumstance, you may not need a consultant, except perhaps to confirm your findings or to implement the solution.

You need a consultant most when you are in trouble and are unable to identify the problem or to trace the cause.

Difficulty in defining a problem sometimes rests with the person who is looking at it. Are you too close to the problem to recognize it? Are you unable to gain a perspective on the situation as a whole? Are you so wrapped up in details, crisis management, personalities, and vested interests that the problem escapes you?

You need to bring detachment and objectivity to your situation to deal successfully with difficult problems. If you cannot, you need a consultant. Detachment and objectivity are the two great strengths of any good consultant.

Some problems are hard to define because they are complex or subtle. Low profits can be due to poor pricing, ineffective marketing, inefficient purchasing, or labor problems, or to some combination of these factors or others. Causes may also lie in human factors such as morale, motivation, or information flow.

Accurate definition of a complex business problem requires expertise and experience. If you and your managers have that expertise and experience, you may not need a consultant. If you are uncertain, you will probably save time and money by calling a consultant as soon as the doubts arise. It takes very clear vision to discern exactly where to intervene in a complicated business problem. Clear vision, like good common sense, is a scarce quality. But it is a quality that you can expect in a competent consultant.

As we had occasion to observe in an earlier chapter, some of the most intractable problems arise in small businesses that are run by members of one family. Harry Levinson (1971) observes that in such businesses, where more than one member of the family is involved, the "fundamental psychological conflict ... is rivalry, compounded by feelings of guilt ...." Founders, set in ways that worked well in past socioeconomic conditions, may resist changes urged by a succeeding generation, by hired managers, or by external events.

Founders may keep their children in subordinate positions long past the age when they should be independently responsible. Family members who depend on the firm for income may refuse to approve necessary capital expenditures. Siblings may bring childhood rivalries into the business. The practice of nepotism can mean that the business is not employing the best possible people in positions of responsibility.

Levinson makes the point that trouble often comes when a business is not run for its own objective needs and purposes. Personal and family goals can interfere with morale, competitiveness, and profitability. Under such conditions, family members should consider seeking the help of a psychologist or psychiatrist—or process consultant—to work out the problems of rivalry or to find solutions that benefit both the family and the business. For example, a consultant might recommend that the family hire professional managers to run the business, or that they sell the firm. Most consultants would probably agree that such radical solutions are appropriate only when family members cannot agree on an objective managerial approach.

Family businesses often find that what seem *business* problems—difficulties in sales, profits, production, and other areas—are actually symptoms of *family* problems. In such cases, company employees should not be expected to deal with the problems. Involving employees can exacerbate the emotional conflicts at the problems' roots. It provides too many opportunities to point accusing fingers and pick fights. It is far better to hire an objective, unbiased consultant who can gain the confidence of all the parties to the conflict. The consultant's primary task in such a situation is to separate purely business problems from the family conflicts. Then the business and family problems can be tackled separately and effectively.

Once business and family problems have been separated in this way, the family business is on the same footing as any other business. Its business problems can, if necessary, be assigned to an appropriate expert. This brings both family and other businesses the benefits of specialized knowledge, technical skills, intensive experience, and top-level talent that their own people may lack. It can also bring in fresh insights and new ideas that can help a bogged-down company start moving again.

At their best, consultants are innovators, stimulants, and catalysts. Even average consultants can stimulate change, though they may be best used as ramrods to get urgent jobs done on time.

The Association of Management Consulting Firms (ACME) emphasizes that consultants can be of great help to small businesses because such businesses are less able to maintain a permanent staff of specialists. Activities such as product diversification, market research, and industrial engineering can be undertaken by a consultant on a temporary and therefore economical basis. The consultant also has the advantage of having solved similar problems for both large and small companies, and so through the consultant the small company can gain from experience and knowledge that are otherwise not available to it. This is true of both management and technical consultants.

61

MANAGEMENT CONSULTANTS

The function of the management consultant is to advise managers on their business's operating problems. The aim of the consultant is to improve managerial and operating performance by analyzing problems, working out solutions, and instructing managers on implementation. The goal of the consultant is to make things happen. The measure of success is the beneficial change brought about in the client's business. The key to success lies in the consultant's ability to inspire confidence, to communicate a plan of change, and to build understanding of the need for the change.

The management consulting industry has grown very rapidly in recent decades. The reason for the growth is that managers face increasing pressures to improve the competitive positions of their companies in a world in which new technologies offer aggressive innovators a strong edge. Consultants who offer state-of-the-art assistance to managers are more essential to competitive success than ever before.

Modern businesses, large and small, face severe external problems of energy shortages and rising prices, inflation, and government regulation of pollution, safety, and health. Other equally important factors that affect business include shifting population patterns, foreign competition, human rights policies, and changing goals and lifestyles of employees. The most immediate problems of American business come from communication and computer devices that are revolutionizing business methods. In addition, new technologies such as genetic engineering are making possible whole new industries. Management consultants can help in these areas.

THE SPECIALTIES OF CONSULTANTS

All these problems need solutions, and they keep the nation's management consultants very busy. What are some of the more common specialties? Alfred Hunt (1977) has compiled the list we reproduce in Exhibit 4–1. ACME offers a considerably more detailed list in its information bank of over 800 categories of specialization represented among its member firms, beginning with:

Absenteeism ... Accident control ... Accounting machines ... Accounting procedures ... Acoustics ... Actuaries ... Advertising agencies. ...

Some people prefer to think of the consultant's work in terms of the consultant's objectives. Arthur N. Turner (1982) has supervised and studied consultants, and he suggests that they have eight primary objectives:

1. Providing information—and obtaining it by attitude surveys, cost studies, feasibility studies, market surveys, and other research.

2. Solving problems—making purchasing decisions, improving management functions, financial policies, or organizational structure, improving pay, morale, efficiency, communication, and so on.

3. Making diagnoses—tracking problems to their sources.

4. Making recommendations based on a diagnosis—studying the problem, its causes, and internal and external constraints, and finding a workable solution the company can accept.

5. Helping implement recommendations—installing equipment and procedures, training personnel, and so on.

6. Building consensus around and commitment to corrective action—getting the various interest groups in a company to agree both that action is necessary and that the recommended action is worth taking; providing needed information, improving communications, and getting people off the dime.

7. Helping the company's people learn to resolve similar problems on their own in the future—for example, by involving company personnel in the work, and by communicating the value of learning.

8. Permanently improving organizational effectiveness—all of the above contribute to this objective, but the most important contribution may come as the consultant demonstrates by personal example effective motivation and function.

63

Exhibit 4–1   Specialties of Management Consultants (after Hunt, 1977).

General Management

Organization studies

General surveys

Long-range planning

Top management appraisal

Executive compensation

Executive search

Production

Plant layout

Production methods

Time studies

Production scheduling

Inventory control

Materials handling

Equipment maintenance

Plant safety

Marketing

Market analysis

Sales forecasting

Distribution methods

Sales compensation

Finance

Accounting systems

Cost accounting systems

Budgeting systems

Cash forecasting

Financial feasibility studies

Exhibit 4–1 *(Continued)*

Personnel

   Job evaluation

   Wage and salary administration

   Personnel record keeping

   Staff training

   Labor relations

EDP

   Computer surveys

   Feasibility studies

   Equipment selection

   Systems development

   Computer programming

   Computer scheduling

   Employee training

Cost Reduction

   Systems analysis

   Work simplification

   Work measurement

   Incentive compensation

Special Services

   Management science—training

   Management science—applications

   Telecommunications

   Environmental controls

   Transportation—analysis

   Transportation—scheduling

   Resource utilization

THE FUNCTIONS OF CONSULTANTS

It may be useful to break the various lists of consultant activities into the five general functions these business advisers serve: planning, marketing, finance, organization, and human resources. Individual consultants may devote most of their time to only one of these functions, and in the process work toward more than one of Turner's eight objectives.

PLANNING

Planning is a strategic component of management consulting, implicit or explicit in all phases of every project. The best consultants gear all their work and recommendations to a long-range perspective on the client company's future, and they try to get the client and the client's permanent management team to take a long-range view.

The reason an experienced consultant insists upon redefining the problem described by the client (see Chapter 1) is to place that problem in the broad perspective of long-run industry and social trends. Redefining a client problem in a broad context lays the groundwork for creating a long-range plan for the client company, while at the same time helping to devise a solution to the particular problem the consultant was hired to solve.

The quick fix is the cheap solution in the short run but may contribute little or nothing to the future of the company. If you feel you cannot afford a consultant who wants to explore problems in a broad planning perspective, you probably lack either the foresight or the resources to be successful in the long pull.

In "Breaking the Barriers to Small Business Planning," a publication of the Small Business Administration, Roger A. Golde defines long-range planning as the process of systematically thinking about the future of an enterprise as an integrated whole. Golde calls long-range planning a vital tool for competing effectively and for reducing future crises.

Long-range planning provides the guidelines for future decisions, increases the lead-time for making decisions, improves the ability of managers to anticipate the long-term effects of decisions and actions, and lays the basis for efficient use of resources.

Sound long-range planning leads to improved operations because the planning process always highlights areas that need attention.

Small business managers should both learn to do their own planning and make planning a normal part of their management routine. Put into practice what you learned in school, take some business refresher courses, or hire a consultant to be your mentor. Incorporating planning in your management routine could be the most important single step you take in building your business and putting it on the road to growth and prosperity. Whether your plan is written down or not is less important than that you have one. Certainly, your plan need not be formal and elaborate. We agree with Philip Thurston (1983) that a plan is a plan, even when it exists only in your own head.

Golde points out several obstacles that can make planning difficult or impossible. Some business people and managers harbor the fear that planning will reveal more problems than opportunities (perhaps you too prefer the serenity of ignorance to the reality of problems!). Some managers are uncomfortable with the uncertainties of the future and do not believe that planning can influence future events.

The planner will point out that planning is actually a process and that a normal part of planning is the periodic revision of a plan in response to unforeseen events. In any case, you will always be better off with a reference point (a plan) against which to judge the impact of events. A sound plan and planning process provides an incentive to keep up with relevant trends and events. Indeed, a plan helps the manager to tell which trends and events *are* relevant.

Some managers plead a lack of time to plan or a lack of planning know-how. The answer to this excuse is that good planning provides the time to plan and ignorance of planning techniques only requires some effort to correct. Here's how to plan:

1. Set goals and objectives for the operation as a whole and do the same for each component of the operation.

2. Write down specific steps for achieving each goal and objective. (Think of a goal as a goalpost in football; an

67

objective is then one in a series of first downs on the way to the goal.)

3. Assess progress toward the goals and objectives. Revise goals, objectives, and steps as necessary.

Once you have completed the first two steps, you have a plan. The third step is the planning process, and it's easy—once you have planning set up and running as part of your management routine. However, getting a plan established may not be so easy if you have never done it. It may be necessary for you to get a consultant to help you the first time around. Unless you have a very complex organization, you may be able to work the plan and planning process into your management system or personal management routine.

Further consulting help with your plan may be needed (a) if your plan requires expert monitoring, or (b) if the process of keeping the plan up-to-date gets behind or is not working.

Bear in mind that planning is too important an element of management to neglect. Good planning can be your most profitable investment. A good planning consultant will not only help you plan but will train company personnel in the techniques of assessing progress and keeping the plan up-to-date. It is your responsibility to make sure that your managers take seriously their planning functions.

Effective planning must begin within the company. It must consider past and expected growth for the company and for the industry. It must take into account corporate goals, the potentials of the company's structure, the capabilities of the company's managers, the abilities and attitudes of the employees, the financial expectations of the company's owners (growth or income?), the financial status and needs of the company, vulnerability to competition, market share, and the efficiency of the company's information flows. Also, planning must take into account trends in technology, changes in public taxation and regulation, trends in the national and local economy, and community expectations.

Changes in climate can affect planning by changing the location of a business's prime market area. For instance, the world is expected to become warmer—by up to 30 degrees Celsius in northern climes—over the next century due to increasing levels of carbon dioxide in the air. As this happens, the U. S. grain belt may shift into Canada, and many farmers and agricultural businesses will follow it. At the same time, coastal areas may flood, forcing many businesses, people, and even cities to move inland. The problems and the opportunities will be endless.

Changes in the age structure of the population can be an important long-range planning factor for many industries. Since the U. S. population is aging, the market for goods and services for babies, children, youth, and young families is shrinking. At the same time, the market for young professionals and older people is expanding.

What about political events and trends? Wars and revolutions affect supplies of imported resources and the markets for exports, as well as the market for military goods. Even without war, U. S. military spending is growing and will probably continue to expand in the foreseeable future. Thus defense contracts are likely to remain a lucrative source of business well into the twenty-first century. Federal, state, and municipal government budgets are major prospects for companies whose information systems are tuned into these public sources of business.

To protect the future of your business, you need to consider a broad range of factors as a basis of planning. The effort will pay off in improving your company's ability to take advantage of new opportunities and prosper.

MARKETING

Successful marketing is the payoff of good planning. Although every company has people who are responsible for marketing its products or services, it is not uncommon, even in larger firms, for the marketing people to lack all the knowledge and skills they need to do the job effectively. Marketing is an area where consulting assistance can be crucial to profitability The following are consulting specialties in marketing:

- The product: packaging, pricing, design, safety, patents, licensing.

69

- Advertising: media selection, ad design, promotions, samples, premiums.
- Public relations: company names and logos; corporate, industry, employee, and customer images; government relations.
- Sales management: market definition, distribution, employee motivation, information systems.
- Market research: consumer attitudes, test marketing, surveys, market share analysis, competitive and industry studies, raw material supplier studies, advertising impact.

Declining market share can force attention to any of these areas. So can declining profit, increased customer returns, or an episode of bad publicity, such as might come when some nut puts pins in candy bars.

In their book, *Consulting to Management,* Larry Greiner and Robert Metzger (1983) recommend that, whatever the problem, the search for a solution begin with a marketing audit that reviews all aspects of the company's marketing program. The audit, conducted either by a marketing consultant or by an experienced company marketing person, should cover the following areas:

- Marketing strategy
- Long-term marketing plans
- The place of marketing in the company's plans
- The sense of customer identity
- Comparisons with competitors.
- Pricing effectiveness
- Advertising effectiveness
- Product design and packaging
- Salesforce skills, training, management, and motivation
- Customer service
- Use of market research
- Development of new products

The root of a marketing problem and its solution may lie anywhere on this list. It may lie beyond the list, perhaps in poor quality control or in bad publicity. The outcome of the marketing audit, if competently done, should yield the answer as well as a plan for solution.

FINANCE

Finance problems often require the attention of an outside expert. A consultant should be called in when a company is experiencing serious cash-flow problems or is unable to meet its capital needs. A consultant should also be brought in when careful, objective attention to financial matters might shed light on other critical problems such as unsatisfactory sales performance. Greiner and Metzger (1983) recommend that the consultant begin the search for answers in the finance area with such questions as these:

- How does the company make money? Is the key factor a unique product, customer loyalty, high sales volume, cost efficiency, high traffic locations, high quality and low costs, a stream of innovative products?
- What does the company do with its earnings? Does it reinvest in plant equipment, hold reserves for future needs, pay generous dividends?
- Does the company use its financial resources efficiently?
- Is the company a risk-taker or a risk-avoider in its financial management and strategies? Are its cash flow and capital sufficient for its future needs? Does it have reserves of credit? Does it use its financial leverage?
- How effectively does the company's financial arm operate? Are its financial people competent and their techniques sophisticated? Does financial information reach managers when they need it?

The answers to these questions are interrelated, and the answer to one of them may hold the solution to a problem raised by another. For example, financial resources may be used more efficiently if they are devoted less to bonuses or dividends than to capital improvement or reserves. The shift may be best achieved by hiring more competent financial managers or by improving information flow.

The financial situation may be so complex that untangling it requires an outside expert. The company's own financial people may be blinded by details or deterred by a vested interest in the status quo.

ORGANIZATION

Organization efforts aim at arranging a company's resources so that goals can be accmplished efficiently. Consultants who specialize in organizational problems try to improve task assignments, the assignment of decision-making authority, lines of communication between people whose tasks are related, and above all accountability for results.

Consultants are necessary in the solution and implementation of organizational problems when managers are reluctant or unable to consider changes that might threaten the scope of their responsibility or even their job. The small business person may simply be ignorant of alternatives to existing arrangements.

Organizational consultants bring to an assignment a thorough knowledge of alternatives. They know how to analyze products in relation to markets and relate the results to company goals. They assess power relationships within the company and how these relationships bear upon success (or failure) in meeting company goals.

The organizational solution recommended by the consultant will give priority to the achievement of company goals over individual and personal goals. The recommendations may urge decentralization to give subordinate divisions increased independence in marketing decisions or in customer relations. They may urge centralization in financial functions such as control over resources and money management. They may urge a regrouping of divisions, perhaps by moving new product development from manufacturing to marketing to improve awareness of consumer needs.

The organizational consultant may work on information flow within the company by recommending a management information system and saying how best to use it for internal communication among company units. The consultant will analyze jobs with the aim of eliminating redundant positions and making other positions more productive and challenging. The consultant will work on short-term tactical planning, goal setting, and budgeting. Experts in organization consider sound budgeting to be the most effective of all organizational tools for carrying out an organizational plan.

The approach consultants employ depends on their training and organizational philosophy, and upon a preliminary assessment of the needs of the client company. The classical school views organizations as pyramids with authority flowing downward from the apex. The organizational principles of the classical school of organization are vertical chain of command, directive control, specialization, and delegated responsibility.

The human relations school, a recent and still maturing philosophy, views the ideal organizational structure as a set of collegial, essentially cooperative (and therefore horizontal) relationships. People work in teams and members contribute as respected colleagues. Team leaders serve as coordinators and as liaison with other teams in the organization. The "top management" team specializes in planning the strategies designed to achieve corporate goals.

The contingency school, to which many practical-minded consultants subscribe, makes use of both the classical and the human relations schools, usually mixing them to achieve workable results. For example, the overall hierarchy is retained as a cohesive structure which preserves the authority of the owners and directors. Within the hierarchy, collegially oriented management teams are formed to achieve high motivation, creativity, flexibility, and rapid decision-making. The team approach works especially well for companies that depend on evolving technologies and changing markets.

HUMAN RESOURCES

Human resource consultants are highly valued among experienced managers. These consultants help companies recruit new employees within the constraints of equal opportunity laws. They assist in improving worker health and safety to comply with state and federal laws. They work on improving motivation, for example by designing compensation plans that cover base wages, fringe benefits, and incentive pay. In such compensation plans, incentives are usually based on performance, fringe benefits on personal needs, and base pay on key job requirements such as skill, knowledge, problem-solving ability, accountability, and working conditions.

Human resource consultants also work on promotion policies, performance appraisal methods, and personnel development and training. These aspects of "people policy" also contribute to employee motivation. They help to ensure a flow of talent toward increasingly responsible assignments.

Executive search consultants help companies fill senior positions and key staff positions. They develop detailed job descriptions and compensation packages, seek and screen out qualified candidates, and introduce the candidates to the company.

On the broadest of levels, people consultants deal in organization development. They study a company's culture, its norms for behavior and their effects on productivity and morale, and they can then identify problems. For instance, they may note that because a company's culture frowns on taking risks, the company cannot retain the sort of people who make risky enterprises work. The new company may then be unable to make new products or new company departments work. Changing such aspects of corporate life is difficult, but it can be done with the aid of a process consultant.

TECHNICAL CONSULTANTS

Technical consultants are specialists in specific, short-term problems. They typically deal with production problems and data processing. They can help evaluate and select equipment, improve the efficiency of a production line, develop or refine a product, suggest product applications, do market research, test product safety, evaluate environmental impacts, improve inventory systems, and prepare reports.

The Professional and Technical Consultants Association

(PATCA) lists 371 consulting skills among its more than 300 members. These skills include the following examples:

accident investigation
appraisals
automation engineering
business ethics
chemistry
computer specialties
copyrighting
cost control
cryptography
education
expert witness
failure analysis

forgery detection
graphics
medical electronics
patent law
plastics
product development
planning, evaluation,
  and safety
radiation
satellite communication
technical writing
warehousing
X-rays

The Association of Consulting Chemists and Chemical Engineers offers an even longer list of specialties for its 120 members. Many overlap with PATCA's list. ACC&CE's list is divided into three parts—consultant functions, materials and products, and process and equipment—to help potential clients find appropriate consultants.

One significant omission from most such lists is lobbying, which is that critical function of representing a company's interests and selling its point of view to legislators and bureaucrats. Much lobbying is done by law firms and public relations firms, but there are individual lobbyists, some of whom call themselves consultants.

An advantage in hiring technical consultants is that they can give a company the benefit of greater expertise and broader experience than most companies can afford on the regular payroll. Consultants of all kinds are exposed to a wide variety of problems in their numerous assignments. Most succeed in keeping their knowledge current. A company employee is likely to have training and experience in a single specialty, whereas by using consultants, a company can employ as needed a series of experts who are specialists in areas such as tax law, patent applications, patent infringements, and lawsuits. By hiring legal consultants, for example, a company can have the equivalent of a large legal staff. The same applies in other areas.

Technical consultants are usually worth hiring whenever a company needs help with a specific problem and cannot afford a full-time employee to do the job. Again, consultants can either supplement or replace company staff. They can meet occasional needs as in market research or plant design. They can supply the leadership and labor for specialized projects, and they can transfer relevant skills to regular employees.

Technical consultants enjoy one great advantage over management consultants. The problems you hire them to address are far more specific. You know when a certain piece of work must be done, and you know what sort of technical expert must do it. The problem lies less in defining the need for a consultant than in finding the right consultant. We take up this problem in Chapter 7.

5

What Does
A Consultant
Cost?

Everyone knows that consultants make a lot of money. Academics jump at the chance to spend a day or two in Washington, with expenses paid, at $500 a day as a fee. Retirees return to their company offices to advise their successors and, for two or three days a month, double their pensions. Full-time consultants live in high style, get around in Lear jets, and drive Jaguars.

Does our tone suggest we are about to say it is all a myth? It is not a myth. Twice a year, Howard L. Shenson, who publishes *The Professional Consultant's Newsletter*, surveys the incomes, billing rates, and business practices of the consulting profession. The Spring 1984 survey published in the April–May issue of the newsletter covered 6,549 consultants of the 69,225 consultants Shenson found to be included on various mailing lists. Among the respondents, the average yearly income was $66,243 (after expenses and before taxes). In some cases, their fees exceeded $1200 a day.

Consultants do not collect big fees every day of the year. They have to spend a large portion of their time looking for new contracts. Furthermore, most consultants have to purchase their own fringe benefits, support an office and staff, and pay other expenses. In the end, full-time, top-of-the-line consultants may earn less spendable income than the managers they serve.

From the client's point of view, the fees look high. Sometimes when managers of small businesses hear of the fees consultants charge, they conclude without further investigation that they cannot afford to hire one. If they need the consultant badly enough, they may try hard to get the fee reduced, either by bargaining or by seeking a consultant with a lower fee. Business people who have had little or no experience with consultants can misjudge the value of the competent ones and make the mistake of opting for what may appear to be a bargain. The bargain rate may not be a bargain at all. What counts, as we shall try to show in this chapter and the next, is the quality of the consultant's work in terms of its payoffs in improved efficiency and profit for the client.

Consultants set their fees according to their income needs, fringe costs, overhead expenses, and—most important of all—the demand for their time and talent. The more their services are in demand, the higher the price on their time.

Exhibit 5-1 shows how members of the Professional and Technical Consultants Association (PATCA) allocate their time. It is on the basis of this allocation of time that they calculate their rates. The allocation includes paid work days, educational seminars, self-education, and administration. As is apparent from Exhibit 5-1, less than 60 percent of the time of a full-time consultant is directly chargeable to clients. Thus, $50 an hour is actually $30 an hour. Forty-three percent of PATCA members earn $50,000 a year or more; 17 percent report earnings of $100,000 or more.

There are comparable data for the consultants surveyed by Shenson. He reports that in early 1984, on the average, consultants were able to bill 57.6 percent of their time to clients. They spent 23.6 percent of their time on marketing their services, 5.7 percent on professional development, and 11.8 percent on administration.

80

Exhibit 5–1 Billed Time Versus Unbilled Time.

Consulting Field

Category and percent reporting	Billed (95)	General and administration (86)	Promotion and marketing (83)	Self-education and seminar attendance (80)	Other unbilled time (48)
Total	59	9	11	8	12
Marketing	59	8	11	5	21
Product	47	10	20	8	10
Engineer	61	10	8	8	12
Program	69	6	8	7	8
Management	52	8	16	6	17
Service	52	8	19	15	9
Other	53	14	11	8	11

From the *1983–1984 PATCA Annual Survey of Consultant Rates and Business Practices.* Reprinted by permission of the Professional and Technical Consultants Association.

Some consultants increase their incomes by boosting their rates. Rate increases usually occur as the reputation of the consultant improves and as his or her skills come into greater demand. Consultants also increase their incomes by adding to the clients they serve and by billing higher proportions of their time to clients. Some consultants—35 percent of PATCA members—adjust their rates to match their clients' ability to pay.

This chapter discusses the methods consultants use to charge for their services. These methods include the common per diem arrangement, flat rates, bracket rates, contingency fees, retainers, deferred payments, and other less common methods. We also discuss available data on actual consulting fees and expenses. We note in closing that *free* consulting services are also available.

PAYMENT METHODS

The Per Diem Fee

Many consultants charge for their services on a per diem or hourly fee basis; Shenson found that 36.3 of his subjects used this method on their most recent jobs. Teams of consultants usually charge per day or per hour separately for each member of the team, the amount depending on individual value. The hourly or daily meter runs while the consultants work, but with rare exceptions, a consulting agreement should include an overall estimate and budgetary limit for the job. An experienced consultant can almost always make an accurate estimate or tell the client if (and why) an accurate estimate is not possible.

During the period of the work, the consultant has an obligation to keep the client informed of any projected budget overrun that would be chargeable to the client. Likewise, the consultant should keep the client informed of revised cost estimates in the case of an open-ended agreement.

An alternative to a set hourly or per diem fee and overall budget agreement is the *bracket fee.* In this arrangement, the consultant estimates the cost of a job within a stated range. The conditions of fluctuation—potential job complications or job elements that may need to be added or subtracted—should be carefully spelled out. The experienced consultant can at least identify such conditions even if their occurrence cannot be accurately predicted. Dishonest consultants can use per diem agreements, without set limits, to overcharge the unwary client.

Per diem fees are useful for brief or intermittent assignments; for billing for the services of the consulting firm; and for advisory sessions with clients. Per diem fees are also a basis for calculating a flat-fee contract.

The Flat Fee

The flat-fee arrangement is appropriate in cases where the consultant can make an accurate estimate of time, expenses, and overhead. The flat fee is not a sound contractual arrangement on jobs where unforeseeable complications might occur, unless carefully drawn contingency clauses are included.

A flat-fee contract has the advantage of giving the client a fixed budget. It has the disadvantage (to the client) of tempting the consultant into rushing a job that is running longer than planned. True, the consultant should never rush the completion of a job at the expense of a quality result. But neither should a client press a consultant to accept an inflexible contract *against the advice* of the consultant. As with any contract, *both* parties have an obligation to place desired results over unsound economies.

Another advantage to the client of the flat-fee (fixed-price) contract is that it permits the client to put the contract out for bids. The Shenson survey found that 28.1 percent of consultants had used a fixed-fee contract and 20.5 percent had used fixed-fee-plus-expenses on their most recent jobs.

Flat-fee contracts are appropriate for straightforward assignments such as studies, surveys, and diagnoses. They are not practical for complicated and unpredictable jobs such as implementing organizational change, for training people, or for installing procedures or complex equipment.

Flat-fee contracts are common in all kinds of consulting work for governmental units, which are obliged by law to use competitive bidding and are constrained by fixed budgets. The disadvantages of the flat-fee contract apply as much to government contracts as to private ones. The frequent occurrence of cost overruns in federal government contracts is stark testimony to this fact.

The percentage contract is related to the flat-fee contract and is frequently used in contracts with architects and engineers. The federal government places a limit on these contracts of six percent of construction costs, so that the fee varies with the size of the project. The American Consulting Engineers Council is working to get the 6 percent limit raised, perhaps to 10 percent, on the grounds that it is too small for complex, small, and

83

rehabilitation projects. The Council may succeed in its efforts, for the federal government has recognized that inequities exist. In fact, it is common for federal agencies to overpay on one project to make up for a contractor's losses on another.

The Retainer

When a company feels it must have periodic help of a specific kind, say in personnel, training, marketing, or human relations, it may retain a consultant to be on call as the need arises. The fee in such an arrangement is a retainer, usually a set amount paid monthly to the consultant. The consultant is available to the client up to an agreed-upon number of hours or days each month. Services beyond that time are charged to the client at the contractual fee.

Retainer fees are usually less, 20–25 percent less, than the consultant's normal fee. Thus the client enjoys a cost advantage so long as the company can use all of the guaranteed time. The consultant enjoys the advantage of predictable income and a client whose problems are familiar. The disadvantage to the consultant is in time limits for new business and in reduced income.

The consultant's objectivity toward the retainer client can in the long run be affected, a disadvantage also for the client. Nevertheless, many independent consultants actively seek retainer arrangements with favorite clients.

The Deferred Payment

A variation on the above payment arrangements is the deferred payment plan used, by and large, with smaller or financially troubled clients who are unable to pay all at once a sizable consulting bill. The deferred payment plan is also used to spread out the cost of consulting to match the flow of benefits from the consultant's work.

The consultant who accepts a deferred payment agreement takes some risk. If the financially troubled client goes bankrupt or the anticipated benefits never materialize, the client may not pay. Consultants who have had experience with deferred payment plans usually set the fee at a higher-than-normal rate to compensate for the risk involved.

Contingency Fees

Contingency fee agreements are usually tied to some measure of the results of the consultant's work. One version is the fee-plus-bonus arrangement which gives the consultant an extra payment depending upon results. A bonus may also be paid when a consultant manages to save a company from failing. Another contingency scheme calls for payment of a fee that is determined by the amount of money the consultant gains for a client in taxes, sales, profit, or payroll.

A problem with contingency fee arrangements is that they can appear to reflect a lack of client confidence in the consultant. It is mainly for this reason that few reputable consultants accept contingency fee arrangements. As we have noted, some professional organizations prohibit contingency fees in their standards of professional conduct. Nevertheless, the Professional and Technical Consultants Association reports that 18 percent of its members use contingency fees and gain an average 10 percent of their income from this source.

A legitimate contingency arrangement is some form of equity in the client company which the consultant is offered as a result of a long-term, successful retainer relationship where the consultant's contributions have been major ones. A different kind of contingency fee appears in cases where the consultant can show that his efforts are so important as to justify a higher fee than the consulting agreement specified. An example would be an exceptionally successful product design, or an exceptionally successful solution to a poorly operating production line. The demand for an increased fee in such circumstances is professionally acceptable only if the client is in full agreement without pressure of any kind from the consultant or if the contingency of exceptional success was discussed and agreed upon during contract negotiations.

EXPENSES

The consultant's time is not the only cost a business incurs when it engages a consultant. There are separate charges for travel, lodging, meals, office expenses, editing, graphics, printing, telephone bills, computer time, research assistance, and supplementary consultants.

These expenses are a substantial portion of the budget of consulting contracts. The big consulting firms bill the time of their consulting staff at about three times actual salaries. For example, they may charge $350 per day for the services of a $30,000-a-year consultant. The difference goes to profit and overhead. Overhead includes time seeking other contracts, cost of facilities, training programs, and services. It does not include out-of-pocket expenses, which can average 10–20 percent of the per-diem fee. These expenses are often billed separately.

Smaller firms and independent consultants have lower overhead expenses and bill their services as a lower multiple of their consultants' salaries. Out-of-pocket expenses remain at 10–20 percent of per diem rates, but they rise when a consultant must hire outside help to do work that is covered in a large firm's overhead. When possible, the client should arrange for the consultant to use company resources: staff, office space, and support services. This practice is thrifty and, since it exposes company employees to the consultant's approach and methods, the arrangement serves to transfer some of the consultant's expertise to them.

Allowing a consultant firm to provide all support services can be expensive, for the rates the consultant applies to nonconsulting services may be considerably higher than the rates of companies that specialize in such services, or than the costs of such services within a client company. In addition, some consultants add a mark-up, averaging 18 percent among PATCA members. (The mark-up for materials averages 20 percent; for air travel, 4 percent; for local travel, 2 percent; for overhead, 2 percent.)

Negotiations with a prospective consultant should include a detailed listing of what expenses are covered by the fee and which are to be separately billed. In some agreements—and usually in flat-fee contracts—expenses are included in the fee. Many consultants include overhead and local travel in their per- diem rates; most bill materials and long-distance travel separately.

The Shenson survey revealed that 44.2 percent of respondents billed time in travel at normal consulting rates; 17.1 percent billed travel time at a reduced rate; 30.4 percent did not charge for travel time. For actual travel expenses, 17.6 percent used a direct receipt/reimbursement basis; 72.9 percent used a per diem plus transportation basis; 9.5 percent did not charge for travel expenses. During the negotiating stages of a new contract, 30.4 percent of respondents charged for both time and travel; 26.5 percent charged for expenses but not for time; 0.7 percent charged for time but not expenses; 42.4 percent did not charge.

The Shenson survey defined overhead as "all indirect expenses which the consultant/consulting practice incurs to maintain operations . . . expressed as a percentage of direct labor (daily labor rate)." Overhead averaged 89.4 percent for the consultants surveyed, ranging from 55.2 percent for the lowest 20 percent to 136.9 percent for the highest 20 percent.

Exhibit 5–2 lists the various factors that contribute to overhead. The largest single factor is the expense of finding new clients—marketing. Other major factors are "practice management" and administration, professional development, clerical support, employment taxes, and personnel benefits.

DOLLARS AND CENTS

The consulting profession has no standard fee structure. Some consultants charge in each contract whatever the traffic will bear, that is, whatever a client is willing to pay for their experience and reputation. Others set rates according to their competition. Jobs that require competitive bids force interested consultants to adjust their rates to win the contracts, although few deliberately undercut their colleagues.

Large consulting firms are as a rule the most expensive, billing consulting time at about triple the salaries of their staff. Smaller firms bill at two to two and a half times salaries. The smallest firms and independent consultants, those consultants with the least overhead, bill at the lowest multiple. If the client's

Exhibit 5–2   Overhead Components

Area/Category of Expense	Percentage
Clerical support services	9.3
Office rent	4.7
Telephone and postage	4.9
Automotive	4.2
Employment taxes	11.2
Personnel benefits	9.8
Insurance	0.8
Business licenses and taxes	0.5
Professional development expense	5.5
Dues and subscriptions	1.1
Printing and photocopying	1.3
Stationery and office supplies	1.3
Accounting and legal	1.1
Practice management/administration	10.2
Marketing	26.0
Other	8.1
Total	100.0

Reprinted with permission from *The Professional Consultant Newsletter,* copyright 1984, and published by Howard L. Shenson, 20121 Ventura Boulevard, Woodland Hills, California, 91364.

needs do not require the facilities and services of a large firm, the smaller firms or the independents can be the economical answer.

Large firms often assign teams of consultants to a job, especially if the client is a large company or the job is a complex one. A team may consist of one or more junior consultants at $250–$300 per day; an associate or senior consultant at $300–$400 per day; and a partner at $500–$1,000 per day. The client should always insist that personnel who are included in the contract actually participate in the job.

It is all too common for partners to appear on the bill even when they were not on the job. Senior consultants may restrict their role to selling the client and subsequently to supervising junior consultants. The client has a right to demand the quality of work that the consulting firm promises in the contract.

Smaller firms usually have fewer junior consultants on their staffs. The senior consultants do the work. They put smaller teams in the field, and hence their per-person fees may be smaller. Thus smaller clients may provide better service at a lower cost, and smaller clients should consider them.

The cost of a consultant also depends on the consultant's specialty. Consider the 1984 daily billing rates in Exhibit 5-3. The average billing rate for all consultants was $674. By specialty, the average rate was lowest for consultants in the areas of fashion and beauty ($443), records management ($458), and recreation ($442). It was highest for those in science ($797), research and development ($736), international business ($747), and health care ($744).

The most expensive 10 percent of all consultants in the Shenson survey billed over $1,200 per day, on the average. The most expensive of these consultants were in international business ($1,293), science ($1,306), investment advice ($1,303), finance ($1,244), advertising ($1,240), health care ($1,175), construction ($1,132), marketing ($1,193), executive search ($1,184), and business acquisitions and sales ($1,107). The least expensive of the top 10 percent of consultants were in arts and culture ($705), grantsmanship ($681), and recreation ($659).

The least expensive 10 percent of all surveyed consultants billed $337 per day, on the average. Arts and culture and records management were lowest in this category at $219 and $228 per day respectively. Construction rated highest at $521 per day.

There is a broad range of consultant fees. The top ten percent and the lowest ten percent in a given specialty can differ by as much as $800 per day. The differential can be as little as $400 per day and it averages about $500. The differentials can be explained in terms of sizes of consulting firms and the reputations, experience, and specialties of their consulting staffs.

Consultants with inferior credentials and experience may try to charge fees comparable to those of better qualified consultants. It is the responsibility of the client to check out the reputation and cost of a prospective consultant before a contract is signed. The objective is to select a consultant whose capabili-

Exhibit 5–3 Average Daily Billing Rates of Consultants, Surveyed by Specialty

Field of Consulting	All	Top 10%	Lowest 10%
All Consultants	$674	$1,226	$337
Advertising	703	1,240	417
Agriculture	514	770	249
Aerospace	681	879	494
Arts & cultural	462	705	219
Banking	602	1,001	436
Broadcast	633	974	489
Business acquisition/sales	629	1,107	358
Chemical	606	878	484
Communications	496	769	252
Construction	642	1,132	521
Data processing	680	1,027	451
Dental/medical	706	959	404
Design (industrial)	581	801	387
Economics	652	956	439
Education	489	705	258
Engineering	723	910	458
Estate planning	638	1,007	411
Executive search	594	1,184	436
Export/import	690	1,014	510
Finance	701	1,244	399
Franchise	606	969	470
Fund raising	552	855	350
Grantsmanship	484	681	336
Graphics & printing trades	513	868	328
Health care	744	1,175	483

Hotel/restaurant/club	547	762	401
Insurance	519	801	311
International business	747	1,293	501
Investment advisory	590	1,303	312
Management	677	1,122	335
Marketing	659	1,193	358
Municipal government	517	710	249
New business ventures	537	998	264
Packaging	624	920	405
Pension & estate planning	662	917	444
Personnel	559	958	326
Production	617	952	458
Psychological services	601	920	289
Public relations	522	912	279
Publishing	540	888	302
Purchasing	545	987	366
Quality control	659	899	395
Real estate	489	1,094	236
Records management	458	801	228
Recreation	442	659	275
Research & development	736	1,255	451
Scientific	797	1,306	517
Security	542	929	330
Statistical	563	886	317
Traffic/transportation	604	933	352
Training	539	871	347
Travel	486	811	256
Fashion/beauty	443	792	240
Retail	609	956	271

ties *and* costs match the proposed assignment. At the same time, clients should not pick consultants whose abilities and prices exceed their needs.

Additional information about costs of consultants is available from the *Annual Survey of Consulting Rates and Business Practices* prepared and published by the Professional and Technical Consultants Association. The 1983–84 edition reports that the average PATCA member charges $53.40 per hour or $427.20 per day (the standard consulting day is eight hours). The average goes up with experience. Consultants with less than three years experience charge an average of $50.70 per hour; those with four to seven years charge $52.90; those with eight years or more, $58.

The rates also rise with the size of the consulting firm and with the consultant's age. The number of consultants whose rates exceed $60 per hour rises sharply for those over 35 years old and for those in firms with two or more members. Independent, single consultants are the least expensive: 27 percent charge less than $40 per hour and 37 percent charge $40 to $50 per hour.

The rates of PATCA members also vary with their specialties. They average $52.50 per hour in marketing; $64.90 in production; $52.50 in engineering; $43.10 in programming; $71.60 in management; $50.80 in service; and $61.60 in "other." PATCA's statistics are consistent with the figures in Exhibit 5–3, although we should note that most PATCA members are based in Northern California and that they do most of their work in the computer hardware and electronic equipment industries. In addition, they focus on the small business end of the economic scale, with 16 percent of their clients doing less than $2 million of business per year and 32 percent doing $2–25 million per year.

CUTTING COSTS

If your business's budget cannot tolerate the burden of a professional consultant, there are alternatives. One is to follow the literature of business, for leading consultants often publish articles describing recent successful assignments. The articles may contain valuable insights on business methods and innovations that pertain to your problems. Consultants write about their work partly to advertise their successes, expertise, and availability.

If you have diagnosed your company's problem, and you come across a consultant's solution to a similar problem in a similar company, you may have found without cost all the help you need. Be warned, however, that taking a solution from the literature is the same as adopting a packaged solution devised for a different company, possibly with different internal circumstances. You or someone on your staff should study the found solution in light of your company's character and circumstances to make certain that it really fits. You may need to adapt the solution carefully to make it work for you.

You may also save money by talking to colleagues in your industry. If competition is not a factor, they may be able to give you the same advice a consultant would sell. Here too the advice you get should be carefully evaluated.

Another course is to hire a reliable and knowledgeable person who does not consult for a living but who is willing to provide advice for a token fee. Such people can be found on the faculties of nearby colleges and universities. We discuss this suggestion fully in Chapter 7.

Still another source of inexpensive consulting help may be found among retired business executives. They may be friends or friends of friends. A very good source is members of the Small Business Administration's Service Corps of Retired Executives (SCORE). These volunteers help small businesses free of charge. The SCORE program is also discussed in Chapter 7.

We caution that free or low-cost advice can lead to more problems than it resolves. While it is possible to minimize the cost of problem-solving, the prudent course when you are in trouble is to bite the bullet and hire a proven consultant. As we have pointed out, the cost can be minimized by careful attention to selecting the consultant and to defining the assignment. If you have a small firm, bear in mind our earlier point that consulting costs can be minimized by choosing a small consulting firm or a reputable individual consultant. For the sake of economy, you should look first in your local area.

If you are in trouble, you should view the price of a good

consultant as a sound investment. Experience among reputable consultants and their clients has shown that the result of a good consultant's labors is to increase a company's profitability by considerably more than the cost of the work.

6

Are Consultants Worth the Money?

Consultants are expensive. They charge up to $1,300 per day, and sometimes more, for looking at a situation, identifying a problem, and recommending a solution. They may also guide the effort to implement the solution.

If they are worth their price, the results of their work save the client many times the cost of their services. The expensive consultants are not the ones who charge the most but the ones who cost more than their services return to the client.

We observed in Chapter 2 that you need a consultant (1) if your business is in trouble and you are unable with confidence to identify what is wrong; or (2) if you know what is wrong but cannot see the solution; or (3) if you have the solution but cannot implement it.

The inability to identify or to solve a problem may be no serious threat to young companies with a new, unique, or high-margin product. But any company that faces aggressive competition cannot afford mistakes and inefficiencies.

Once it is clear that outside expert help is needed, the

decision to retain a consultant should be based upon a hard-headed assessment of the probable gains over the estimated expense. In many cases, this initial assessment will benefit from preliminary expert analysis, and such help at this stage could avoid a faulty and expensive choice of the wrong consultant.

Consider: The average consultant costs $674 per day plus 20 percent in expenses. If a company engages a consultant for two weeks (10 working days), the consultant's bill may be as much as $8,088, a sizable item in the budget of a small or troubled company. For a publisher, this sum could represent the royalty advances necessary to acquire three or four new titles or the cost of printing and binding one book. For the manufacturer, it could be the cost of a new machine tool or testing instrument. For the office operation, it could be the cost of a high-efficiency computerized work station.

Could the money be better spent in one of these other ways? It is rarely possible to know for sure whether the decision to spend money on a consultant is a sound one until after the consultant has come and gone.

Hiring a consultant can be risky for a small business. There can be no guarantee of a profitable result. Yet, if you *are* in trouble, you should seek competent help.

Consultants do not usually promise results. What a reputable consultant does promise is recommendations based on hard facts, careful analysis, and good judgment. Bear in mind that it is up to you, the client, to evaluate the reputation and record of the consultant *before* you sign a contract.

Do not choose a consultant on faith alone. Justify your choice of a consultant with as much care as you would any other business decision. The penalty for failure to do so is the risk of bankruptcy.

Unfortunately, some consultants would prefer that you be trusting. Some experts insist that a consultant is worth his or her fee if, once the assignment is complete, the client feels good about the experience and would repeat it willingly. While this statement may be true in many cases, it is not a rule that you should take seriously if you have had little or no previous experience with consultants. It certainly does not allow for distinctions between the consultant who adds genuine value to your company and the ingratiating con artist.

Others say that a consultant earns his fee by fulfilling the terms of his contract with you, the client—performing tasks, fulfilling responsibilities, meeting deadlines, writing reports, and achieving goals. Deciding whether a consultant will actually live up to such contractual terms is in fact an important part of evaluating a consultant, and we will discuss it in Chapter 9.

However, even a consultant who does everything he or she has promised can be a waste of money, if the client-consultant contract does not include some statement of purpose. The consultant's recommendations, *once implemented,* should have a direct, measurable impact on your financial situation. If they do not, the consultant is not worth the fee.

The consultant's profession is strongly based on knowledge, on facts, wisdom, and insight. Yet too many consultants do seem to say, "Trust us. Of course we are worth hiring. We wouldn't be in this business if we weren't." Sometimes they actually seem to discourage attempts to put a dollars and cents value on their efforts, as if they feared the results of such evaluations. This fear may be the real reason why many consultants are reluctant to work on a contingency basis. They may worry that, if their fees depended on real financial benefits, those fees would be too small.

Yet not all consultant assignments can be evaluated objectively. Process consultants, who focus on improving human interactions, may leave behind little more evidence of their success than intuitive feelings of reduced conflict or smoother operations. "Yes, things have been going better, morale is up," may be the response of a previous client to an inquiry. Only if the process consultant has been able to reduce wasted time in unproductive or counter-productive interactions can an actual dollar figure be placed on the effort.

SHORT-TERM IMPACTS

Survey and "action" assignments can be rigorously evaluated. Does the consultant begin work at the time agreed and does the consultant stick to the contract schedule? Fuchs (1975) emphasizes that adherence to a time schedule is especially important if a large number of people are involved, as in a task force, profit-improvement plan, or strategic business plan. Fuchs observes that a client company with a well-defined profit planning approach must monitor program slippage because slippage can affect budgetary commitments, deployment of key personnel, and other internal controls.

The consultant's ability to keep costs within budget is especially important to the small-business client. The consultant should never increase the scope of a project or the time devoted to it without the client's agreement. The consultant should never add any costs without the client's consent. The uncontrolled consultant can balloon the cost of a project beyond the ability of the client to pay.

It is important to consider whether the consultant's presence will disrupt the flow of work within the client company, an especially important consideration in small companies. Disruptions caused by an outsider can seriously impair productivity, sales, and profits, possibly to the point of offsetting the value of the consultant. Whenever serious disruptions occur, they impose hidden costs for the use of a consultant.

Consultants can take undue employee time in interviews and conferences, and they can require large amounts of clerical services. Experienced consultants time their interruptions of work for minimal impact. For instance, interviews can be scheduled for slack days and slow business seasons. Experienced consultants also keep their demands for clerical help within reason. For instance, they request photocopies only of selected, pertinent documents, not of the entire company archives.

Some consultants have much more potential than others for disrupting or not disrupting work. Labor relations consultants, for instance, can resolve union problems without work stoppages, but only if they are sensitive to worker feelings and get a timely start on the problem. Production consultants can minimize—or maximize—the time a production line is down. Computer consultants can manage a smooth transition in management information systems—or leave a system in complete chaos for weeks. Personnel consultants can fill vacant positions quickly—or slowly. Training consultants can teach new skills in weeks—or months. Tax and legal consultants can meet penalty

100

deadlines—or miss them. Fund-raising consultants can make goals—or fall short of them.

The consultant to choose is the one with a verifiable record of limiting the direct and indirect costs of services. The consultant to choose is the one who produces tangible, measurable results. Unfortunately, while the results may show up right away in improved production, improved profits may not be evident until the year's end. We call such delayed benefits mid-term benefits.

MID-TERM IMPACTS

Income and Expense

Improvements in the client company's financial position may be demonstrable improvements in sales; in dollars spent per unit sold; in reduced costs for raw materials, purchased items, or finished product; in labor costs, shipping costs, or warehouse costs; in reduced sales returns and allowances; or in overhead. The consultant may have found that the market will tolerate a higher product price. The consultant may have improved market research, advertising specificity, or sales force training. The consultant may have found cheaper materials from which to make the product or a supplier whose efficient shipping arrangements reduce the need for maintaining large inventories. The consultant may have broadened product mix or markets to avoid dependence on seasonal markets. The consultant may have smoothed work flow, introduced automation to reduce the workforce, increased labor productivity, improved use of work space, reduced costs of handling materials, or reduced the number of people required to back up manufacturing or sales.

Such changes and improvements show up in the company's statement of income and expenses. They provide data for evaluating the work of a consultant. They also provide numbers that can be projected to show the consultant's long-term value to the business.

Consultants whose efforts pay off for the client justify their time by returning benefits worth many times their costs in actual

101

dollars and cents. The benefits can be so large that some highly paid consultants can rightly claim that their fees are irrelevant, that their clients are investing tiny amounts against large returns. The fees look enormous only to clients who find it difficult to believe in the benefits.

Not all consultants are so effective. It is crucial that prospective business clients check carefully into the past performance of any consultant under consideration.

If a consultant with a good record nevertheless fails to deliver, the problem may lie with the client's inability to use the consultant's advice. For example, when new technology is rendering an entire product line obsolete, the consultant may advise developing new products or entering a new industry. Such a change may not be possible if the company lacks the necessary human, capital, or credit resources.

The Balance Sheet

The client company's balance sheet is not often used for evaluating consultants. It should be. This invaluable financial tool displays the status of and changes in such aspects of the company's business as cash flow, accounts receivable and payable, inventory, and fixed assets. Consultants can help in each of these areas. They can develop procedures to reveal cash flow and to predict available cash for short-term expenses, investments, and capital expenditures. They can devise methods to forecast cash flow for future needs. They can assist in short-term and long-term planning. They may be able to increase the interest income on cash investments.

As valuable as such benefits can be to a client company, there are other less measurable benefits that can be provided by the consultant. Such benefits include, for example, the consultant's experience and foresight to take advantage of opportunities that had not previously been seen or had to be passed over.

Consultants may also be able to develop improved methods of appraising the credit-worthiness of customers, reduce the number of outstanding accounts, shorten the period between billing and payment, reduce bad debts, or improve the efficiency and effectiveness of collecting delinquent accounts. In each case, the consultant can reduce the amount of interest lost on unpaid bills and in the process improve the company's income.

With accounts payable, the consultant may be able to extend the time the company has to pay its bills and thus increase the number of days it can earn interest on its money. The consultant may increase the number of cash discounts from which the company can benefit, develop methods to ensure meeting payment terms, and organize a system to receive, inspect, approve, and store incoming shipments.

Inventory shows up on both the balance sheet and the statement of income and expense. The consultant may be able to keep inventory of raw materials and finished products to a low level. The result will be reduced cash expenditure, reduced warehousing expense, and reduced loss to obsolescence or limited shelf-life. The end result can be reduced accounts payable, less idle time in production, and cash available for short-term or long-term investment.

What can a consultant do about fixed assets? Consultants can help companies decide whether to lease or to buy capital equipment; whether to make parts and subassemblies or to contract their manufacture; how to time and manage purchase of capital equipment (in terms of investment tax credits, depreciation, cash requirements, obsolescence, and short- and long-term requirements). In this area, the consultant's impact can translate into dollars available for other uses and also into actual savings

LONG-TERM IMPACTS

The financial results of the consultant's efforts can project far into the future. These long-term impacts may be literal extensions of the short- and mid-term impacts we have already discussed. They may differ in that they become visible later rather than sooner, but not necessarily in how long they last.

Other long-term impacts are more qualitative. While working for the client company, the consultant works with the client's employees. The consultant may lead a team investigating problems or developing methods. Or the consultant may only confer with the company's top executives. Either way, the consultant's way of looking at problems and working out solutions is on display. The best consultants seek to teach their approaches; they also teach some of their expertise.

After the consultant has gone, the approaches and knowledge should remain with the personnel of the company, available for application to future problems. Thus the best consultants increase their clients' problem-solving abilities by deliberate modelling and transfer of skills and knowledge.

Consultants serve as leaders as well as educators. They increase the abilities of client company personnel by encouraging those with whom they work to perform to the limits of their potential. They motivate company personnel to push the company toward growth, to sell aggressively, and to compete effectively. In the process they seek to improve attitudes and to raise morale.

The achievement of beneficial change is the ultimate function of the consultant. In the role of catalyst for change, the successful consultant strengthens management's capabilities, stimulates development of sound methods for formulating policy, clarifies areas of authority and responsibility, optimizes communication within the company, and specifies workable operating systems, procedures, and assignments.

It is rare that a consultant leaves a client company with a permanent capability to solve all future problems. Even the most successful consultants can do no more than *improve* the client company's functioning. Even the best consultants have to return periodically to make adjustments and to deal with new problems.

The ideal consulting arrangement from the standpoint of both the client and the consultant thus is a long-term relationship, perhaps on a retainer basis, renewed annually. Under such an arrangement, the consultant has the obligation to keep track of the client company's condition and prospects, internally and externally. The consultant is in a position to advise management on corporate strategies when an acquisition, merger, or divestiture is under consideration. The consultant can assist in the development of long-term and short-term profit plans. With in-depth knowledge of the company's functioning, capabilities,

104

objectives, and aspirations, the consultant on retainer can be invaluable in advising on response to developments in the industry and in the public sector.

This set of observations brings up the question of why a company should not hire a full-time staff consultant instead of an outside one. In some cases, a staff consultant is a practical, effective, and economical arrangement. But in the vast majority of cases, a staff consultant is more expensive than one on retainer for the reason that most companies need consulting advice for only a few days a year, once the in-depth work of the initial problem-solving effort has been accomplished.

A staff consultant must be paid all year long whether advice is needed or not. Management may feel it must assign the staff consultant other responsibilities, and those other responsibilities may get in the way of the staff consultant's efforts to prepare for and deal with problems that may arise in the company. A major disadvantage of a staff consultant is inevitable involvement in company politics and the lack of objectivity and perspective so crucial to the solution of both internal and external problems.

The outside consultant, on the other hand, brings a wealth of experience gained from other assignments as well as the objectivity and motivation of the self-employed professional.

The staff consultant is justified in very large companies with numerous, complex, rapidly changing problems. Such companies benefit from the internal consultant's detailed knowledge of the company's structure, history, and capabilities. Even there, an outside consultant may often have to be called in to work in tandem with the staff consultant to lend objectivity and perspective in situations where substantial change may be necessary.

SURVEY VERSUS ACTION ENGAGEMENTS

In its booklet on *How to Get the Best Results from Management Consultants,* by Philip W. Shay (1981), the Association of Management Consulting Firms (ACME, Inc.) breaks consulting engagements into two types. *Survey* engagements focus on client problems and recommend solutions. *Action* engagements aim at getting results for the client. Action engagements may include improvement of market penetration, development of new products, and strengthening of research capabilities.

The work of consultants in both types of engagements should be evaluated according to whether the engagement's purpose, scope, procedures, and terms are properly planned and the type of result that is expected is explicitly stated. In either case, consultants should abide by the agreed-upon schedule and budget and should work constructively with client personnel. Principles, methods, skills, and techniques should be transferred to client personnel.

An important objective of the consultant in this context is to help the client organization through the client's own personnel to understand and use recommendations, to make changes work, and to minimize the need for future consulting engagements.

Recommendations should be complete, timely, practical, effective, economical, and above all suited to the client's needs. They should also take into account client policies, plans, and capabilities with due consideration for the human element. The consultant's results should embody the best collective judgment of the consultant and the client's own people.

At the end of the engagement, the consultant should explain all findings, conclusions, and recommendations to those client executives who will be responsible for evaluating and implementing them. The consultant should also emphasize the importance of careful planning in preparations for putting the recommendations into operation. The consultant should offer to assist the client in their implementation.

All of these factors must be considered when the client evaluates a consultant's performance. In addition, the client must consider which of the consultant's recommendations were accepted and used and which were rejected, which actually worked, and how well the company performed during the engagement. Did the work with the consultant improve the competence of company personnel? Finally, the client should consider whether it is satisfied enough with the consultant's efforts to engage the consultant for a future assignment.

Several additional factors should be considered in evaluating

106

the results of action engagements. The action consultant should coordinate development programs with the client's purposes and objectives and match them with company resources and potential. The consultant should explore reasonable alternatives with the client before committing the client to a specific and irrevocable course of action.

In urging a particular course of action, the consultant should demonstrate technical competence and flexibility for adapting to changing circumstances. The action consultant should assist in the design of organizational modifications and procedures needed in the successful implementation of recommendations.

A program of implementation, once settled upon by the consultant and client, should accurately and realistically account for company resources as well as its strengths and weaknesses. The program of implementation should help the client to make moves efficiently, minimize wasted motion, and provide lead-time for future moves. The end result should improve client teamwork, communications, operations, and profits. Company executives should be satisfied that the new ways recommended by the consultant are improvements over the old. If they are, the consultant was surely worth the cost of the engagement.

The best measure by far of the worth of a consultant is the dollars and cents results as reflected on the books of the client. The consultant who is willing to give the client his or her honest best judgment regardless of the client's willingness to accept it is in the long run preferable to the consultant who compromises to gain the client's good will.

Consider the case of one company, run by an aging founder in the habit of making decisions by whim and instinct. The company was fast losing ground to its competition, and the founder's income was declining. Eventually the founder called in a consultant who, after careful study and analysis, said, in effect, "Retire. Hire a professional manager and live off the income he generates for you. Keep your incompetent mitts off the show."

In making the recommendation, the consultant was aware that his advice might be rejected and the company lost as a future client. Yet the founder listened, and the company prospered. The only unhappy result was that the founder was separated from a life-long commitment.

THE HUMAN ELEMENT

The ACME booklet notes that a consultant should consider the human element when devising a solution to a client problem. This does *not* mean always agreeing with the client's prejudices. It does mean considering the client's needs while discounting dysfunctional habits of operation and prejudices. It means focusing on the health and welfare of the business and taking into account the human needs of the people involved. It means devising solutions that the company's people can work with and accept. It means finding answers that fit the client's corporate culture.

The most successful and desirable consultants generate solutions that never would have occurred to their clients. Again, the key to success in gaining acceptance of their solutions is the deliberate involvement of company personnel in the research, investigation, analysis, consideration of alternatives, and selection of the program of action. The result is a solid commitment of company personnel to the solution and to its effective implementation because they believe the solution is their own. The "not invented here" syndrome never arises.

There are situations in which the client does not need a specific solution to problems. The client may already have a workable idea but may lack the confidence or capability to implement it. In some cases, contending factions within the company may have created a stalemate. Here the consultant's role is to provide information, expert judgment, and support for the client's plan. The consultant's role, if he can do so in good professional conscience, may be no more than to confirm the soundness of the client's plan.

When Richard D. Irwin founded the publishing firm that still bears his name, he planned it carefully. He defined a market and a product—business textbooks—with which he was familiar. He estimated demand and growth more optimistically than other publishers. Though it was during the Great Depression, people wanted business training to improve their chances for getting scarce jobs; that meant business textbooks. Irwin was determined and confident. Nevertheless, he turned to consultants before he launched the business. The men he consulted were friends, authors, and business professors, and their opinions of his plans strengthened his confidence. He went ahead with the plans, and his confidence was boosted even more when his consultants paid *him*, investing in his new business.

Finding the Consultant You Need

In previous chapters, we have discussed the varieties of consultants, their cost, and their value, and how to decide when and whether you need one. In this chapter, we discuss how to go about finding and choosing a consultant.

Careful selection is important. The intensity of competition in the consulting industry can have the effect of discouraging cautious, reflective comparison. The business person who has decided to hire a consultant should devote the time to check background, competence, and especially references. Hasty selection can lead to serious mistakes. Hasty clients can wind up with hasty, superficial consultants, too many of whom populate the fringes of the consulting industry. Such consultants exist because the industry is not unified and therefore has no consistent standards. It is easy for almost anyone to open an office and put "consultant" on the letterhead.

On the other hand, not all people who have something to contribute toward solving business's problems call themselves consultants. There are a considerable number of knowledgeable people around who rarely or never engage in consulting. We will label such people "nonconsultants." These are experts in their respective fields who are not formally in consulting, either because they do not care for the full-time consultant's high-pressure, far-travelling life or because their main interests lie in other activities. We include such people in our discussions here because many of them have much to contribute to businesses that need help and, as we shall see, some may have a great deal to offer at a modest cost.

FINDING "NONCONSULTANT" EXPERTS

Experts who are not consultants may not be very interested in consulting, in some cases, because their main concerns take up most of their time and in other cases, because their basic income is sufficient for their needs. When these "nonconsultants" do consulting, it is because someone has sought them out and persuaded them that the problem they are asked to solve or the project they are asked to work on will contribute to their knowledge, experience, and notoriety in their field of interest—and the fee is large enough to be attractive. It is the combination of these incentives that lures such people into a consulting job.

Most of those people we call nonconsultants are experts who work for universities. They are somewhat easier to attract to an assignment than experts who work in industry because their salaries are usually lower and they are usually free to do with their time as they wish. Experts who work in industry may be more highly paid and not as free to take on outside projects without clearance from superiors. The industrial experts may cost more than professors. Some university-based experts do not make themselves available as free-lance consultants because they are either on retainer to a corporation or government agency or "on call" to some high government policy official.

The nonconsultants are hard to get, but they should not be overlooked as a potential consulting resource. Among them are some of the outstanding experts in their respective fields. They may be much more knowledgeable in a problem area where your business needs help than some full-time consultants. They are worth seeking out and asking for help. Some nonconsultants have gone into consulting as a consequence of having been lured to projects that whetted their intellectual and monetary appetites.

Some "nonconsultants" may be far less expensive than full-time consultants for the reason that they may not have any overhead. Professors are usually privileged to use university staff and facilities for outside projects so long as they can demonstrate that the work is related to their teaching duties and research interests. One common trade-off in universities is jobs and experience for students on the consulting projects of faculty. Industry-based nonconsultants may not have overhead if they use their homes or offices for spare-time projects.

Where can expert nonconsultants be found? As we have already suggested, they are in universities and in large corporations, banks, and financial houses. Retired specialists are another source. (Do not try to hire staff members of consulting firms for "spare-time" work. The staffer who would take the job is violating the trust of the employer and should not be considered trustworthy.)

The first place to look is on local campuses. The faculties of colleges and universities include people who teach courses in every area of business, including finance, planning, marketing, and technology. Many of these people are doing research at the forefronts of their fields, and what they know may not yet have reached the full-time consultants. The older such people are, the more likely they are to have established a consulting practice, but younger faculty are frequently available, almost certainly up-to-date in the state of the art of their field, creative, eager, and inexpensive. A young expert on a university faculty can be a very good bargain.

The better the university, the better the bargain, partly because young faculty persons probably have free access to top-drawer experts at the university in case they need advice. Graduate students can be valuable (and very inexpensive), and some university courses use real-life business problems as student projects. If your problem got to be a student project, it could also get the thoughtful (and perhaps free) attention of an experienced professor.

At smaller schools, the faculty may include fewer experts in business-related fields and less research may be going on. Nevertheless, the faculty who do teach business subjects know their fields and can help businesses find answers to their problems. The faculties of small colleges may be in less demand as consultants than their colleagues in the universities and therefore not as expensive. For your purposes, there can be some real bargains among them. As an example, one small—500 students—business school in Maine devotes its faculty efforts solely to teaching, but most of the faculty members share their expertise with small businesses in the area. As a service to the business community, the college has a staff person who refers inquiries to the appropriate faculty members.

Business schools are not the only academic source of help for businesses. Medical schools can assist in matters of worker safety as well as health and environmental impacts. Liberal arts faculties can help with planning, projections, economics, and technical issues. Law schools offer legal expertise. Police academies may be especially valuable when it comes to security matters.

Many schools have set up mechanisms to help businesses find aid among their faculty members. Some larger schools take their efforts to be helpful even further. The University of Wisconsin has a Small Business Development Center (602 State Street, Madison, WI 53703) which publishes a journal, the *Wisconsin Small Business Forum,* and the *Wisconsin Business Resource Directory,* a compendium of local sources of business help, including county extension agents, local consultants, state agencies, financing sources, and publications. Other state universities provide similar help, and it is worthwhile for any business to check what is available in its own state. State development offices may have useful publications. Maine's *Doing Business in Maine* is one example.

Still another source of nonconsultant expertise is the U.S. Small Business Administration. It runs four major programs, in financial assistance, management training and counseling, securing government contracts, and advocacy. It provides a great deal of help in free and low-cost pamphlets. It also sponsors SCORE, the Service Corps of Retired Executives.

SCORE provides free business consulting by volunteer retired executives who have had successful business careers in large corporations or as proprietors. They share their knowledge and experience to help businesses improve operations or get established from scratch. SCORE is a nonprofit public agency and the retired executives who participate as consultants are unpaid volunteers.

SCORE has upwards of 400 chapters across the country and it has more than 11,000 volunteer consultants on its rolls. The national office of SCORE is at 1129 20th Street, Suite 410, Washington D.C. 20416 (202-653-6279). Local offices are listed in telephone books under SCORE, U.S. Government, or Small Business Administration.

You may also find experts among retired business people by asking personal and business friends, bankers, accountants, attorneys, and the local Chamber of Commerce. Such people may also be able to steer you to other business people who are willing to share their experience and knowledge: free-lance writers who can prepare reports; noncompetitors who have faced similar problems; and men and women who have shifted careers from business to some other pursuit.

You can also find help by paying attention to magazine and journal articles, books, reports, and speakers. The guest at a Rotary Club luncheon may be just the expert your business needs. Do not hesitate to draw the interesting speaker aside after the speech to find out if he or she is available for an exploratory conversation or exchange of letters.

A book, article, or report may display exactly the expertise your business needs; if so, you should contact the author about your problem. In most cases, you will get a sympathetic hearing. If the expert is not available or cannot help, he or she will probably give you a lead to someone who can.

You may wonder if we, the authors of this book, might be able to help with a problem. The answer is yes. We can probably help if you are having a problem finding the right consultant or if you are having trouble defining a problem. These are among our areas of expertise. We can also help with planning, policy

117

development, trend analysis and direction, innovative approaches to marketing of products and services, and technical writing and editing.

If you decide to contact authors of books, articles, and reports that seem relevant to your needs, you should be prepared to provide all available information that bears on your problem. Reputable consultants keep all such information confidential. As a precaution, you should ask the expert to maintain confidentiality on matters that in your judgment require it. Once the issue of confidentiality is settled to your satisfaction, you should share with the expert all the relevant facts as well as your own interpretation of them as guides in a preliminary assessment of the problem. If you are thorough in your description of the problem, its factual basis, and the conditions surrounding it, the expert might be able to come up with some possible answers. At the very least, you will provide a solid base from which to proceed with an analysis.

FINDING CONSULTANTS IN DISGUISE

It is common for companies that sell computer hardware, software, technical instruments, carpeting, or other products to say, "Let our customer consultants analyze your needs and recommend the perfect solution!" The "perfect solution" always turns out to be the company's own product, or a solution that requires the use of a company product. Company consultants lack one prime characteristic of the true consultant: objectivity. Company consultants are actually salespeople in thin disguise, even when they charge a fee for their services.

There are situations in which it can pay the customer to consult such people. Salespeople must know what their company's product can do as well as what it cannot do. They must be able to offer sound advice on the best and most efficient uses of the product. This is especially so in technical areas. The good ones also know the competition's products and will go so far as to recommend one for a use their own company's product cannot serve.

Valuable as customer consultants can be in informing their

clientele about the products they sell, it behooves the customer to judge whether (a) the product can meet his or her needs, and (b) whether the product is the best one for the purpose.

The astute customer should talk to "customer consultants" of several companies to compare products, prices, support services, and quality of advice about applications.

Consultants in disguise are also people who are not consultants at all but who help business in their role as discerning consumers. Eric von Hippel (1982) reports that the semiconductor industry gains two-thirds of its machines from users. The scientific instrument industry gains 80 percent of new instruments from users. A third of all software IBM leases to users of its large and medium computers comes from the company's own customers. IBM actually runs an Installed User program to find and acquire outside software. Pillsbury finds new products via the Pillsbury Bake-off contests that began in 1949.

In addition, gardeners develop new varieties of flowers, vegetables, and fruits. Craftspeople design new special-purpose tools. Physicians as medical researchers develop new diagnostic procedures and treatments. Von Hippel points out that customers often develop their own products when suppliers decline to do so because of too small a market. Once the product exists, an unexpected demand for it can be created, sometimes when an alert journalist introduces it to an interested public.

Customers sometimes develop original products or adaptations of existing products when they want the competitive advantage of exclusive use or application. Alert companies can sometimes buy the rights to such products. Companies can also listen when their customers describe their needs and then develop suitable new products. It is for this reason that forward-looking companies maintain close relations between their marketing and product-development departments.

It is often cheaper for a company to acquire customer-developed products than to initiate a new product from scratch. Von Hippel recommends that companies take advantage of this option by defining the products they want as precisely as possible. Suitable incentives and rewards can then be offered as inducements to consumers who are capable of responding. The incentives might include research grants, royalties, prizes, and offers

119

of outright purchase. In order to save screening costs, initiating companies should inform only the likely product sources of the list of desired products and of the incentives.

An alternative to the "user stimulus" strategy is the "user analysis" strategy. Here, the company deliberately and systematically considers which customers are likely to develop products. It can then go to the customer with an offer. Scientific instrument companies exploit this strategy extensively in scanning the scientific literature for early, sometimes fragmentary reports of new techniques and devices.

An important obstacle to using customers as product sources is the negative and sometimes self-defeating policy of some companies that can be described as the "not invented here" attitude. Such companies believe they should concentrate their "new product" efforts on product ideas that are initiated within the company. Other people's ideas are ignored or regarded as unpromising. A shift from this attitude can be a profitable change if the shift is accompanied by an aggressive program to search for new product ideas outside the company.

Still another variety of consultants in disguise can be found on corporate boards of directors. Board members are usually chosen because of their expertise in some aspect of the industry or a business skill, their perspective, or their analytical ability. Board members serve as overseers, and collectively they have some authority over company managers. But their most valuable function, if brought into play, is the advisory one—in effect, consulting.

Small business owners ordinarily prefer to have family, close friends, and business associates serving on their boards. These are usually the people who have provided the capital to start or continue the business. From the standpoint of board members as advisers, close friends and associates may lack the independence and objectivity to be of great value when serious problems arise.A popular alternative in circumstances of crisis is the "quasi-board," a group of independent, objective, knowledgeable outsiders whose only assignment is to evaluate management performance and give advice (Fox, 1982). Universities call them visiting committees.

A quasi-board lacks a real board's legal power and accountability, and its members are paid less than regular board members—$500–$1,000 per session, high "enough to establish an obligation of diligence but low enough to preserve the member's autonomy" (Fox, 1982). The members of quasi-boards are chosen for experience, ability, and willingness to contribute; they are managers from larger companies, bankers, noncompeting business people, technical specialists, consultants, professors, customers, suppliers, attorneys, accountants, and psychologists. Quasi-boards may meet three or four times a year, or less, but they can be very valuable, serving many of the functions of professional consultants. Fox cites several examples:

- A quasi-board member tipped the company president to a public relations firm that helped him become an industry spokesman.
- A quasi-board helped beat problems of cost overruns, shipping delays, and salespeople's dissatisfaction by suggesting a job-order and project accountability system.
- A quasi-board noted that a business owner's plans for expansion were poorly defined, lacking estimates of future sales; the owner dropped the plans in favor of other, more viable plans.
- A quasi-board persuaded an over-extended owner to cut his business in half; the result was immediate profitability and better planned growth from a sound base.

Other quasi-boards have helped evaluate applicants for executive positions, ease conflicts between managers, and optimize reward systems. They have done everything for which a business might hire consultants, and they have often served at considerable monetary savings. One drawback is that time is required to select and organize an effective quasi-board. Sometimes members have to be replaced. The overall process can resemble the development of a management team or the selection of a consultant.

FINDING PROFESSIONAL CONSULTANTS

Professional consultants derive all or most of their income from helping businesses with problems. They are easy to find. They head their own consulting firms or they work for one. They are

121

listed under "Consultants" in the Yellow Pages of the telephone directory. They advertise their services. They belong to various professional associations which publish directories of their members.

Computerized consulting has become a high-tech reality. Stonehedge Information Services has developed the Geneva Series, accessible through CompuServe (P.O. Box 20212, Columbus, Ohio43220, 614-457-8600), as a way for small businesses to reach and deal with large consulting firms. Any business can get the Geneva Series password by paying CompuServe a $100 annual subscription fee. The subscriber may then use a personal computer and modem (telephone converter) to tap a data base listing 100 consulting firms and services.

The subscriber may search the data base according to the category of assistance required—management, law, and finance are examples—and examine the personnel lists, credentials, reports, and fees of the consulting firms. Once the subscriber has located the appropriate consultant, he can deal directly with the consultant through the computer. The service was set up and offered to subscribers in 1984, and thus it is too new for us to report on its effectiveness.

The problem many business people face in seeking a consultant lies not in finding one but in finding one who is competent and right for a particular job. The care put into the search is the best means of assuring success in the job. Most of the search must be devoted to screening, evaluating, and comparing candidate consultants.

The effort is least when you learn of a consultant through the enthusiastic recommendation of a business associate, friend, magazine article, or book. The effort is greatest when you pick a candidate consultant blindly from a directory or advertisement. The effort may be just as hard when the consultant initiates the contact. An initial recommendation from a trustworthy source makes all the difference.

The first rule in finding a consultant is never try to hurry the search and screening process. It is too easy to make a costly mistake. The choice should be from among two or three finalists, each of whom has submitted a preliminary plan and budget. Antony Jay (1977) recommends that you have someone else draw up the final list of candidates. He points out that the research necessary to match consulting expertise with your business's needs and to check a consultant's references can be tedious and time consuming. The temptation is to short-cut or rush the process. Jay emphasizes that successful consultants thrive according to their ability to impress potential clients and that a person other than the client may be better able to see past the charm and persuasion to the true competence for the job.

The evaluation process should include systematic consideration of the following eight factors:

1. Reputation
2. Performance history (track record)
3. Areas of specialization
4. Previous clients
5. Experience of previous clients with the consultant
6. Interview analysis
7. Quality and relevance of proposal
8. Performance of preliminary (trial) assignment

CHECKING REFERENCES

Philip W. Shay (1981) recommends that potential clients refrain from checking references in detail until the candidate consultants have been winnowed down to one or two. Each candidate should be able to name several (more than one) satisfied past clients. No consultant should be given serious consideration who refuses to name any past clients. Experienced consultants know that reference checks protect both the client and the consulting profession.

The person who checks references should be an executive or consultant who understands the nature of the proposed assignment and the results the client expects to achieve. The face-to-face interview with reference sources yields the most reliable basis for evaluation of the sources.

The wisdom of using professional assistance at the screening stage of consultant selection becomes apparent in the evaluation of reference sources. If a source company's president was

123

satisfied with the consultant's work but the middle managers were not, this may be an indication that the consultant's recommended solution was impressive but unworkable; or that he or she is unable to work with "peons"; or that he produced an unpopular result that was nevertheless exactly what the president intended. A careful probe in such circumstances almost certainly requires the skills of a professional to yield a result that is both fair to the candidate consultant and of maximum value to the prospective client. Are we recommending a consultant to help select a consultant? Yes, we are.

Shay lists ten questions that should be asked in detailed reference checks:

1. What was the nature of the consultant's work?
2. Did the consultant show professional competence, objectivity, and integrity?
3. Did the consultant work constructively with the client's people?
4. Did a senior consultant give the work adequate supervision?
5. Were the results complete, timely, practical, and tailored to the client's specific needs?
6. Were recommended actions optimally effective and economical from the client's point of view?
7. Did the consultant stay within budget and on schedule?
8. What impact did the consultant's work have on client function?
9. How did client executives view the overall value of the consulting engagement?
10. Would the client engage the consultant again for a similar assignment?

The reference check should include a credit rating, an interview with the local Better Business Bureau, and an interview with the candidate consultant's banker.

The most important single criterion in selecting a consultant is relevant experience, especially demonstrable skill and success in solving problems similar to the one at hand. A thorough professional evaluation of specific, similar problem-solving experience is the key. The consultant's own description of past projects is never a sufficient basis for the evaluation. Exaggeration or misplaced emphasis can intentionally or unintentionally distort the reality of past experiences. Written backgrounds may highlight aspects of experience or education that have been selected to fit the prospective client's particular needs but fail to reflect the consultant's true strengths—or weaknesses. Past clients, for reasons of confidentiality, may be described elliptically ("major players in the industry"). But the prospective client needs to know, indeed has a right to know, precisely who the previous clients were, at least verbally.

In addition to past clients, the consultant has also worked with other professionals: accountants, architects, and builders, for instance. Some of these people should be interviewed. The prospective client may subscribe to a trade journal, and the editor may have some useful comments on consultants who regularly work in the industry.

The consulting profession has few widely recognized certification procedures and standards of professional behavior but, as we pointed out in Chapter 3, some groups to which some consultants belong do have and do enforce such procedures and standards. From the client standpoint, hiring a consultant who belongs to one of these groups is added assurance of quality, reliability and, most important of all, integrity.

THE INTERVIEW

A crucial part of the evaluation process is the interview with the candidate. It is best to do the interview only after the candidate has had an opportunity to study the prospective client's written description of the problem at hand and the result the client expects to achieve. Preparing the description helps in selecting candidate consultants, who in turn must have the problem description as a guide to presenting their qualifications and preparing a preliminary proposal.

Interviewers should pay careful attention to how well the candidate listens to questions. They should ask the consultant for a brief preliminary analysis of the problem under discussion and for some indication of the approach the consultant would use in seeking a solution. The candidate should be encouraged to suggest a reformulation of the problem if he or she appears inclined to do so. (There are occasions when a consultant's most important contribution is in a reformulation of the problem as presented by the cient).

PROPOSALS

The finalists should be invited to submit formal proposals. The proposals should state the consultant's understanding of the problem and description of the work to be done, the methods to be used, and the specific results to be achieved. They should express project goals in concrete terms: bolster faltering sales, install a new compensation system, design a management information system. Proposals should never promise specific dollar savings. Consultants who make such promises are likely to overstate their capabilities in other ways as well.

The proposal should detail the qualifications of members of the consultant's firm who would be assigned to the job. If the list does not include the consultant with whom the client has discussed the job, the client should make a point of meeting and evaluating the members of the firm who are on the list.

The client should also be sure that those who are listed will actually work on the project and with what assignments. Note that junior members of the firm may lack experience and expertise and therefore may require the close supervision of a senior consultant. The quality of supervision should be an important determinant in selecting a consultant who proposes to assign junior staff members to the job.

A good proposal should also outline the background and expertise of the consulting firm as a whole, describe the firm's available resources, and list some of its past clients and projects. This information helps the potential client evaluate the consultant's suitability for its needs.

Finally, a good proposal should provide a schedule for the work to be done, specify the times for progress reports and interim evaluations, and spell out the cost of the consulting services as well as the method of payment.

Dexter and Schwab (1975) emphasize that a business person faced with evaluating several proposals from consultants should not necessarily choose the one that promises the least total cost. A far more important criterion is the promised benefits of the consultant's labors per dollar of cost. They caution that low bidders may finagle changes in the job description and schedule. Such changes can lead to serious cost overruns.

This may happen when the candidate consultants think that the cost of the contract is to be the principal factor in the client's selection of the successful bidder. Low bids can result in cost overruns when it is too late to take corrective action, or they can result in short-cuts that affect the quality of the work. The search for cheap and easy solutions to complex problems can cause trouble.

Antony Jay's (1977) caveat should be heeded: "Never take on an untried consultant for a project that could make or break the whole organization." If you want to hire an inexperienced consultant, take the precaution of making the assignment to a portion of the larger project or to a smaller trial project.

A consultant who does well on a project may be worth a long-term relationship. Such relationships offer the advantage of having a valuable and trustworthy expert who can be called upon without going through the time-consuming process of a search. These relationships have the added advantage that the consultant becomes thoroughly familiar with the business and can approach new problems with less preparation and therefore less expense. The long-term consultant may also have a strong interest in the health of the business. A drawback is that it may prove difficult for the consultant to maintain objectivity and independence. Also, prolonged dependence on a consultant may discourage management from assuming appropriate responsibility for maintaining internal efficiency.

Once you have chosen a consultant and approved a proposal, it is time to consider how to get the most from the engagement. We discuss this topic in Chapter 9, "Getting Your Money's Worth." Chapter 8 is a compendium of consulting sources included here for your convenience.

8

A Catalog of Consultant Sources

Consultants are easy to find. All that any business needs is the admission of need, the knowledge that they exist, and a list of the professional associations to which many consultants belong. These associations often serve as clearinghouses, and anyone may call them for referrals to consultants whose specialties may serve a business's needs. The next steps involve evaluating the referred consultants, selecting finalists, and inviting proposals, as discussed in Chapter 7.

Earlier in this book, we mentioned the Geneva Series, which anyone with a personal computer can access through Compu-Serve (P.O. Box 20212, Columbus, OH 43220, 614-457-8600); it provides a way to examine the specialties and qualifications of 100 different consultant firms for a modest cost, and then to deal directly with these firms via the computer.

We also mentioned the Small Business Administration's Service Corps of Retired Executives (SCORE), whose 11,000 volunteers provide free assistance to small businesses. Its national office is at 1129 20th Street, N.W., Suite 410, Washington, D.C. 20416, (202-653-6279).

In this chapter, we will concentrate on the professional consultants' groups, summarizing the activities of their members, describing available publications, and giving addresses and phone numbers.

Our list of consultant groups in this chapter is *not* exhaustive. Other groups exist as well. However, those listed here do cover a broad range of consultant specialties. Whatever a business's needs, at least one of these sources should be able to provide help.

AMERICAN ARBITRATION ASSOCIATION

With 60,000 members, the AAA is the largest of the national groups of conflict-resolution specialists. The other groups include the:

- **Conflict Resolution Center**
  7514 Kensington Street
  Pittsburgh, PA 15221
  412-371-3607

- **Institute for Mediation and Conflict Resolution**
  116 East 27th Street
  New York, NY 10016
  212-685-4400

- **National Academy of Arbitrators**
  4335 Cathedral Avenue, N.W.
  Washington, D.C. 20016
  202-686-1140

- **National Academy of Conciliators**
  5530 Wisconsin Avenue, Suite 1250
  Washington, D.C. 20015
  301-654-6515

- **Society of Maritime Arbitrators**
  26 Broadway
  New York, NY 10004
  212-483-0616

- **Society of Professionals in Dispute Resolution**
  1730 Rhode Island Avenue, N.W., Suite 509
  Washington, D.C. 20036
  202-296-8510

Many of the AAA's members are psychologists. All work to resolve disputes and personality conflicts in business. They are often called in when one party to a dispute activates a contract clause that calls for binding professional arbitration, perhaps even specifically for AAA mediation. Fees depend on the sums at stake in disputes.

The AAA makes referrals through its National Panel of Arbitrators. It publishes several monthly reviews of arbitration events, the bimonthly *Arbitration Times,* the quarterly *Arbitration Journal*, and assorted pamphlets and manuals. Contact the organization at:

- **American Arbitration Association**
  140 West 51st Street
  New York, NY 10020
  212-484-4000

AMERICAN CONSULTING ENGINEERS COUNCIL

ACEC's 3,800 members are self-employed engineers. The organization publishes an annual membership directory and a separate *Minority Directory,* as well as a newsletter for its members. ACEC strives to improve its members' capabilities in public relations, business practices, government affairs, codes, and other areas, and it compiles statistics on its members' businesses. Contact the ACEC at:

- **American Consulting Engineers Council**
  1015 15th Street, N.W.
  Washington, D.C. 20005
  202-347-7474

AMERICAN SOCIETY OF AGRICULTURAL CONSULTANTS

ASAC's 300 members are business and technical consultants who specialize in serving the needs of agriculturally related

133

businesses worldwide. Its aims include maintaining high standards of ethics and competence among its members. It runs a referral service, and it publishes irregularly a newsletter. Its address is:

- **American Society of Agricultural Consultants**
  8301 Greensboro Drive, Suite 470
  McLean, VA 22102
  703-356-2455

AMERICAN SOCIETY OF CONSULTING PHARMACISTS

This organization's 1,700 members are registered pharmacists and educators. Most focus their concerns on the needs of health-care facilities. The organization compiles data, maintains a speakers bureau and an information file, and publishes quarterly and monthly newsletters. Its address is:

- **American Society of Consulting Pharmacists**
  2300 Ninth Street, Suite 503
  Arlington, VA 22204
  703-920-8492

AMERICAN SOCIETY OF CONSULTING PLANNERS

The 1,500 members are involved in city, regional, and other planning programs. The organization compiles statistics, sponsors research, and publishes an annual directory, a newsletter, a Code of Professional Conduct, and pamphlets. To contact it, write or call:

- **American Society of Consulting Planners**
  1717 N. Street, N.W.
  Washington, D.C. 20036
  202-659-2908

ASSOCIATION OF CONSULTING CHEMISTS AND CHEMICAL ENGINEERS

ACC&CE's 120 members are chemists and chemical engineers involved in consulting to businesses of all sizes that need help in product formulation, product testing, production, and many other areas related to the manipulation of substances. They subscribe to a Code of Ethics, and ACC&CE has a Professional Welfare and Ethics Committee to which alleged unethical behavior can be reported. The organization publishes the *Your Consultant Newsletter* and the *Consulting Services Directory of Members* (22nd Edition, 1984) and their specialties. It also operates a central clearinghouse which answers inquiries from prospective clients and makes referrals to ACC&CE members. The Association's address is:

- **Association of Consulting Chemists and Chemical Engineers, Inc.**
  50 East 41st Street, Suite 92
  New York, NY 10017
  212-684-6255

ASSOCIATION OF EXECUTIVE SEARCH CONSULTANTS

AESC has 61 member firms specializing in recruiting managers at salaries over $35,000 and agreeing to abide by strict standards of professionalism and ethics. The organization publishes quarterly reports of collected statistics, guidelines, brochures, and a list of members. To contact it, write or call:

- **Association of Executive Search Consultants**
  30 Rockefeller Plaza, Suite 1914
  New York, NY 10112
  212-541-7580

ASSOCIATION OF FEDERAL COMMUNICATIONS CONSULTING ENGINEERS

AFCCE has 150 members who practice before the Federal Communications Commission. Their concerns are both engineering and the allocation of broadcasting frequencies. Their aim is to promote federal administration of the engineering and technical aspects of radio communication. They have no publications.

- **Association of Federal Communications Consulting Engineers**
  P.O. Box 19333
  Washington, D.C. 20036
  202-659-3707

ASSOCIATION OF GRAPHIC ARTS CONSULTANTS

AGAC has 50 members, each with at least two years of experience as a graphic arts consultant. It publishes the bimonthly *Printing Mergers and Acquisition News* and an annual membership directory.

- **Association of Graphic Arts Consultants**
  1730 North Lynn Street
  Arlington, VA 22209
  703-841-8140

ASSOCIATION OF INTERNAL MANAGEMENT CONSULTANTS

AIMC's 210 members are internal consultants, serving the functions of consultants as employees of larger companies. The AIMC publishes a quarterly newsletter and has a committee on ethics.

- **Association of Internal Management Consultants**
  c/o Thorne Perry, Executive Director
  P. O. Box 472
  Glastonbury, CT 06033
  203-633-5826

ASSOCIATION OF MANAGEMENT CONSULTANTS

AMC's 110 members are smaller consulting firms. Its objectives include "To help provide the smaller businessman with competent professional advice at price (sic) he can afford to pay" and "To assist interested organizations, both large and small, in locating qualified consultants by furnishing an annual directory of its members and their services, or by circulating inquiries to its membership" (from an AMC pamphlet). It is thus one of the better groups for small business people to call or write when they seek a management consultant.

- ■ **Association of Management Consultants, Inc.**
  500 North Michigan Avenue, Suite 1400
  Chicago, IL 60611
  312-266-1261

Members of AMC can use the letters AMC on their letterheads. This logo supposedly attests to the member's professional competence and integrity, but all it really stands for is the qualifications for membership: three years of full-time practice as a consultant, successful past performance (reviewed by the Committee on Admissions), "a reputation for honest dealing and integrity," and agreement to abide by AMC's Code of Professional Practice. Members need not demonstrate their competence in special examinations.

In addition to its membership directory, AMC publishes a newsletter and assorted pamphlets explaining AMC and management consulting. It also serves its members in the areas of public and governmental relations and maintains a list of members qualified to speak or write on various topics.

THE ASSOCIATION OF MANAGEMENT CONSULTING FIRMS (ACME, INC.)

ACME's 61 members are larger consulting firms that put much of their effort into larger client businesses, but that also serve smaller businesses. The fees of larger consulting firms, as noted in Chapter 5, tend to be higher. Most member firms provide a broad spectrum of consulting services, though each firm has its own strengths and main activities. The list of ACME members in the Appendix gives only the names of members, the addresses and telephone numbers of their main offices and the locations of their branch offices. Additional information about members is available from ACME at:

- **Acme, Inc.**
  230 Park Avenue
  New York, NY 10169
  212-697-9693 (in California and Texas,
  call 1-800-221-2557)

ACME's Information Bank lists more than 800 activities and areas with which member firms can help. In addition, ACME maintains information on 2,200 nonmember firms.

ACME publications include Philip Shay's *How to Get the Best Results from Management Consultants* (1974, 1981), a free directory of members, a 1983 survey of fees, and numerous reports and bibliographies; most are much less expensive than the $200 fee survey. ACME also maintains a large library, available to members and others, at its New York offices. Its enforced Code of Ethics is among the most elaborate in the consulting industry (see Chapter 3).

ASSOCIATION OF PROFESSIONAL MATERIAL HANDLING CONSULTANTS

APMHC's 34 members specialize in the problems of handling materials in production, storage, shipping, and so on. The organization has a code of ethics, conduct, and qualifications; publishes a semiannual newsletter and a membership directory; and runs a speakers bureau.

- **Association of Professional Material Handling Consultants**
  1548 Tower Road
  Winnetka, IL 60093
  312-441-5920

ASSOCIATION OF TAX CONSULTANTS

ATC's 800 members specialize in matters related to taxes. The organization has a code of ethics and is concerned with education and lobbying. It helps its members find jobs and publishes the quarterly *Tax Times*, a membership roster, and brochures.

- **Association of Tax Consultants**
  P.O. Box 16184
  Portland, OR 97233
  503-249-1040

AUTOMATED PROCEDURES FOR ENGINEERING CONSULTANTS

APEC's 220 members specialize in the use of computer technology for designing environmental systems for buildings. APEC publishes the bimonthly *Journal,* a membership directory, and brochures.

- **Automated Procedures for Engineering Consultants**
  40 West 4th Street
  Dayton, OH 45402
  513-228-2602

CERTIFIED CONSULTANTS INTERNATIONAL

CCI's 340 members use the techniques of social and behavioral science to work in the areas of personal, professional, and organizational development and societal change. The organization has an accreditation process and publishes a quarterly newsletter and an annual membership directory.

- **Certified Consultants International**
  Box 573
  Brentwood, TN 37027
  615-377-1306

FOODSERVICE CONSULTANTS SOCIETY INTERNATIONAL

The 370 members of FCSI advise on layout, management, etc., of food service operations. FCSI publishes the quarterlies *The Consultant* and *Spec Sheet* (newsletter), an annual membership roster, and legislative and regulatory reports.

139

- **Foodservice Consultants Society International**
  1000 Connecticut Avenue, N.W., Suite 9
  Washington, D.C. 20036
  206-362-7780 (Seattle office)

INDEPENDENT COMPUTER
CONSULTANTS ASSOCIATION

ICCA has 1,000 members specializing in computer-related services and products. It provides its members with standard form contracts and business and financial advice. It publishes the bimonthly *The Independent*, the annual *Conference Proceedings*, and the annual *Directory*. It maintains committees on ethics, standards and procedures, and referrals.

- **Independent Computer Consultants Association**
  P.O. Box 27412
  St. Louis, MO 63141
  314-567-9708

INSTITUTE OF CERTIFIED PROFESSIONAL
BUSINESS CONSULTANTS

The function of ICPBC is to certify the members of the Society of Professional Business Consultants as well as members of other consultants' associations. Certification requires five or more years of practice as a consultant to professionals (physicians, dentists, etc.), passage of a rigorous competitive examination (see Chapter 3), and adherence to the ICPBC's Code of Ethics and Rules of Professional Conduct. Certified consultants may use the letters CPBC after their names.

The ICPBC publishes a quarterly newsletter and maintains a registry of all CPBC consultants.

- **Institute of Certified Professional Business Consultants**
  221 North LaSalle Street
  Chicago, IL 60601
  312-346-1600

INSTITUTE OF MANAGEMENT CONSULTANTS

The IMC's *Directory of Members* for 1983–84 lists nearly 1,200 members who are entitled to put the letters CMC after their names, plus about 240 associate members (new consultants not yet qualified to call themselves CMCs) and 75 senior associate members who are inactive or retired CMCs. The CMC stands for the consulting industry's only widely recognized certification program. The certification requires at least five years of full-time consulting experience, with at least one year of major project responsibility; six references, three of them from recent clients; written summaries of five client assignments in which the applicant played a major role, including one very detailed summary; and passage of a qualifying interview that accesses knowledge, skill, and commitment to the IMC Code of Professional Conduct.

IMC members are individual consultants. Many belong to larger firms, which may be members of ACME or AMC, but many are individual practitioners. The IMC is thus a good organization to contact when a small business needs help. For referrals to IMC members or for a copy of the *Directory, Code of Professional Conduct*, or other pamphlets, write or call:

- **Institute of Management Consultants**
  19 West 44th Street
  New York, NY 10036
  212-921-2885

INSTITUTE OF RISK MANAGEMENT CONSULTANTS

The 60 members of IRMC advise business and government on analyzing risk in order to choose insurance (or other forms of security) appropriately. IRMC publishes a directory and six to eight issues of its journal, *The Communicator*, each year.

- **Institute of Risk Management Consultants**
  58 Diablo View Drive
  Orinda, CA 94104
  415-254-9472

141

INTERNATIONAL ASSOCIATION OF
MERGER AND ACQUISITION CONSULTANTS

INTERMAC's 55 members assist in finding candidates for and negotiating mergers and acquisitions in the media, insurance, financial, manufacturing, food processing, and other industries. Membership requirements stress experience and financial ability. INTERMAC maintains a biographical profile of officers of member firms and publishes a monthly newsletter and a membership directory.

- **International Association of Merger and Acquisition Consultants**
  1258 Goodnight
  Dallas, TX 75229
  214-241-0254

INTERNATIONAL ASSOCIATION OF
PERSONAL IMAGE CONSULTANTS

IAPIC is an informational clearinghouse serving 250 member firms who specialize in coaching speech, appearance, dress, and other aspects of image. IAPIC publishes a biannual directory.

- **International Association of Personal Image Consultants**
  c/o Editorial Services Company
  1140 Avenue of the Americas
  New York, NY 10036
  212-354-5025

INTERNATIONAL ASSOCIATION OF
STRATEGIC PLANNING CONSULTANTS

The 180 members of IASPC help business clients with corporate, new venture, and strategic planning. The organization sponsors a data bank and the Strategic Identification Program (Strat-ID) to categorize strategies and predict effects on profit. IASPC sponsors research, compiles statistics, maintains a library, operates a speakers bureau and a referral service. It holds seminars and conferences and publishes the bimonthly *Strategies* as well as an annual membership directory.

- **International Association of Strategic Planning Consultants**
  P.O. Box 5198
  Akron, OH 44313
  216-836-4410

INTERNATIONAL COLLEGE OF REAL ESTATE CONSULTING PROFESSIONALS

RECP's 333 members specialize in giving sales, financial, and other advice to the real estate industry. RECP operates a certification program, and Certified Real Estate Consultants may put the letters CREC after their names. It also conducts seminars, compiles statistics, maintains a library, and runs referral and placement services. RECP publishes a monthly newsletter, two irregularly issued journals, and an annual directory.

- **International College of Real Estate Consulting Professionals**
  305 Foshay Tower
  Minneapolis, MN 55402
  612-665-6282

INTERNATIONAL CONFEDERATION OF ASSOCIATIONS OF EXPERTS AND CONSULTANTS

ICAEC has 72,000 members worldwide who are consultants, experts, and appraisers of all kinds. The organization's goal is to develop a true profession of experts and technical consultants. To this end, ICAEC publishes an *Index of Categories and Specialties of Experts and Consultants.*

- **International Confederation of Associations of Experts and Consultants**
  Seige Adm.
  rue 10 Bosch, 85 Bte 85
  B-1050 Brussels, Belgium

INTERNATIONAL CONSULTANTS FOUNDATION

ICF's 140 members are experienced professional consultants, trainers, researchers, educators, and authors. They specialize in human resource development. ICF has a Committee on Ethics and runs seminars and training programs. It publishes an annual registry, the semiannual *International Consulting News,* occasional books, and other literature.

- **International Consultants Foundation**
  5605 Lamar Road
  Bethesda, MD 20816
  301-320-4409

NATIONAL ASSOCIATION OF PERSONNEL CONSULTANTS

NAPC's 2,400 members work for private employment agencies. The NAPC compiles statistics and certifies members. One of its committees deals with the ethics of the profession. It publishes a membership directory and ten issues yearly of *Personnel Consultant.*

- **National Association of Personnel Consultants**
  1432 Duke Street
  Alexandria, VA 22314
  703-684-0180

NURSE CONSULTANTS ASSOCIATION

NCA's 110 members are registered nurses who consult with industry and business on health issues. In part, members work to improve the understanding of manufacturers' products by

144

health care personnel. The NCA publishes a quarterly newsletter and semiannual membership directory.

- **Nurse Consultants Association**
  1130 Winners Circle
  Libertyville, IL 60048
  312-680-9377

PROFESSIONAL AND TECHNICAL CONSULTANTS ASSOCIATION

PATCA's 300-plus members work as individuals or as members of small firms to supply businesses with technical services in management, computer technology, engineering, marketing, technical writing and editing, and many other specialties.

PATCA has several grades of membership: fellows have demonstrated exceptional competence; members have been full-time consultants for at least one year (or for three of the previous six years) and have submitted three acceptable client references; associate members are part-time consultants or full-time consultants who have been in business for less than a year and have submitted three professional references; affiliate members have only expressed an interest in making a profession of consulting. All classes of PATCA members pledge to abide by the Association's Code of Ethics.

PATCA publishes a *Directory of Consultants* for use by potential clients, and the Association operates a free referral service. PATCA also publishes an annual survey of consulting rates and business practices (see Chapter 6). The Association publishes a newsletter and runs seminars for the business community.

- **Professional and Technical Consultants Association**
  1190 Lincoln Avenue, Suite 3
  San Jose, CA 95125
  408-287-8703

PUBLIC RELATIONS SOCIETY OF AMERICA

The 11,000 members of PRSA are not consultants, but their

145

function can on occasion be similar. They are often called to repair damaged public images, publicize new developments, coordinate advertising programs, and to help with other public relations problems. They work in government, industry, and business. The PRSA operates an executive referral service, a speakers bureau, an information center, and a small library. PRSA publishes the monthly *Public Relations Journal*, an irregularly issued newsletter, and the annual *Public Relations Register*.

- **Public Relations Society of America**
  845 Third Avenue
  New York, NY 10022
  212-826-1750

SOCIETY OF MEDICAL-DENTAL MANAGEMENT CONSULTANTS

The SMDMC's 80 members provide business and financial advice to medical and dental professionals. The Society has no certification program or published code of ethics. It restricts its functions to conducting surveys and compiling statistics, and to publication of a bimonthly newsletter, annual membership directory, and other materials.

- **Society of Medical-Dental Management Consultants**
  4959 Olson Memorial Highway
  Minneapolis, MN 55422
  612-544-9621

SOCIETY OF PROFESSIONAL BUSINESS CONSULTANTS

SPBC is the parent organization of the ICPBC. Its members are consulting firms and individuals who supply physicians, dentists, and other professionals with management advice. Many individual members are certified by the ICPBC. Membership requirements include experience, competence, and dedication to full-time consulting and adherence to the SPBC Code of Ethics.

146

The SPBC publishes a newsletter, an educational bulletin, *The Consultant,* and pamphlets for potential clients. Two of the pamphlets are titled: "Need advice from someone with no axe to grind?" and "Getting the most from professional business consultants." Both pamphlets are intended to explain the functions of SBPC members and promote the marketing of their services. SPBC also helps clients by making referrals to members in their geographical area.

- **Society of Professional Business Consultants**
  221 N. LaSalle Street
  Chicago, IL 60601
  312-346-1600

SOCIETY OF TELECOMMUNICATIONS CONSULTANTS

STC's 91 members are specialists in marketing, manufacture, or distribution of telecommunications products. STC's members also include product designers, electronic engineers, and experts in effective use of telecommunications. The STC has an ethics committee. The Society publishes papers, reports, a quarterly newsletter titled *STC Lines,* and a quarterly membership roster. Businesses that need help in telecommunications should write or call:

- **Society of Telecommunications Consultants**
  One Rockefeller Plaza, Suite 1912
  New York, NY 10020
  212-582-3909

9

Getting Your Money's Worth

The value of the consulting industry is indicated by the thousands of firms and tens of thousands of individuals who are in it. The industry bills more than $3 billion per year, and that sum grows each year. Most clients believe that consultants add more real value to their businesses than they cost.

There are complaints. Even happy clients do not always get all the value they might for their money. The problems lie partly with the consulting industry, but not entirely. Some clients do not know how to use consultants to get maximum value. How to get full value is the subject of this chapter.

Most businesses could gain considerably greater benefits from the consultants they employ by following a few common-sense practices. We have touched upon some of these practices in previous chapters. First, we have pointed out the importance of knowing exactly what you, the client, want the consultant to do and what results you expect. What is the problem? The best consultants will press this question to the point of absolute clarity before they accept a job.

What is the desired goal or change? The consultant can help you answer this question once the problem is clear. In fact your initial answer may not be satisfactory and, as we said earlier, one of the first and often most valuable contributions of the consultant is to help you redefine the problem in such a way as to reveal one or more desirable goals (or changes).

Answers to these first two questions are essential to every consulting assignment, in marketing, strategic planning, taxation, and computer software design, to name a few examples. The answers, carefully and thoughtfully framed, invariably lead to workable solutions. From the consultant's standpoint, the quality of the answers makes the difference between a successful outcome and failure.

Second, it is of critical importance to select the consultant to suit the problem at hand. The chances are that the consultant who, in the screening stage, does the best job of helping you clarify the problem and set goals is the one who is likely to do the most satisfactory job. If the consultant can state the problem clearly, anticipate goals, and identify areas of needed change, this is good evidence that he or she understands the problem you have presented. What better place to begin a project than from a demonstrable understanding of its essentials?

We emphasized in Chapter 7 the practical necessity of a thorough screening procedure—checking credentials, past performance, and relations with previous clients—in selecting a consultant. You must be sure the consultant has the required resources in experience, education, time, personnel, and computers—in short, whatever is necessary for the job.

Screening is tedious and time-consuming and, for these reasons, easy to pass over with quick, superficial checks. But a superficial screening process begs later problems. If you select the wrong consultant, you can expect poor research, sloppy or badly written reports, weak analysis, unworkable recommendations, overruns in budget and time, and perhaps disruptions in the workplace.

If these suggestions sound like general good management

practice, that should come as no surprise. Consultants, like all other aspects of business, must be managed and managed well. The managing of a consultant does not stop with defining needs and selecting one. It continues throughout the consulting engagement, and even beyond. Getting the most value out of consultants means defining the job, facilitating the work, maintaining control, and following through with agreement on a solution and a plan of implementation.

DEFINING THE JOB

When you confront a problem you cannot solve within your company, act promptly to call in a consultant. Do not wait until the problem has caused serious trouble for you and the company. Antony Jay (1977) cites the dramatic case of the British producers who spent $80,000 shooting the first two thirds of a comedy film. Only at that point did they call in two leading comedy writers for advice. The writers bluntly told the producers, "Don't waste your money shooting the rest. It's a turkey." Their $800 fee would have been precisely the same if they had been called in before the shooting began. However, they could then have given the producers two options instead of one. The producers could have cancelled the project before the large investment had been made, or they could have retained the writers to rewrite the script or start again from scratch.

Defining the problem for which you are hiring a consultant should always be a joint effort shared by you and the consultant. It follows that the consultant must be involved at the earliest practical steps in working toward a solution. Once selected, the consultant should be asked to define (in writing) the problem as he or she sees it and to suggest an approach to a solution.

The resulting consultant's statement becomes the basis for discussions between you and the consultant. These discussions should lead to an agreement on the definition of the problem, and the agreement in turn should provide the basis for a concrete plan to find a solution. Close and attentive interaction between you and the consultant is of greatest importance at this stage because the direction and guidelines of the entire project are set here and they largely determine the odds for success.

153

During these early discussions with the consultant, you should seek to understand very clearly what techniques the consultant proposes to use, how they work, and exactly how they will be applied in the project. Generally it is a mistake to allow the early discussions to dwell on technique; they should instead focus on approach. Peterson and Kerin (1980) urge caution against the "technique mystique" trap. A focus on approach helps to ensure that the consultant understands the techniques well enough to use them properly.

The point is that consultants, especially in technical fields, can become enamored with techniques. They may be inclined to experiment with new techniques that glitter with "cutting edge" gold, and with which they may not be entirely familiar. Preoccupation with technique can be harmful to a project. If not held in check, preoccupation with technique can cause time and budget overruns or worse. In a recent political campaign, a computer consultant tried to persuade the candidate to commit voter lists to an untested automatic dialing system designed to use a recorded message to urge the voters to go to the polls. The technique addressed a campaign problem of saturation voter contact, a substitute in a large, heavily populated district for door-to-door campaigning. Since the technique fit the problem, the consultant pressed hard to get the candidate to accept it. The candidate agreed that the technique would reach the voters, but declined to accept it as a campaign approach, pointing out that the personal style that had been the hallmark of the candidate would be seriously compromised with voters who received the recorded message. Campaign funds were running short, and the automatic call system would preempt vital television and radio messages. As it turned out, the consultant had wanted to test the system in a real campaign and placed that objective above other, competing demands on scarce campaign funds.

The client should always reveal to the consultant the real reasons for hiring him. The consultant should know in detail what he is supposed to accomplish. You do your part in the early discussions if you are open and complete in your description of the problems at hand and the goals and objectives of the assignment. If confidentiality is an issue, then the consultant's reputation for maintaining confidentialities should be a criterion in the selection.

The written description of the job should cover not only what is to be done, but also who does what. It should spell out what you and your staff will do to support the consultant. For example, your contribution may include providing office space, secretarial service, and other logistical support.

The job description should also indicate special constraints and instructions, such as staying away from the shipping room staff on Fridays. It should specify schedules, deadlines, reporting dates, methods of evaluation, and payment arrangements.

Once you have the job description on paper, you should review it carefully with the consultant. The final step before work commences is the contract. This may be a signed letter or a memorandum attached to the job description, or it may be a formal document drawn up by legal counsel. Whatever form it takes, the agreement should provide for termination of the engagement should either party become dissatisfied. A penalty clause should be included should either party wish to end the contract for reasons other than substantive ones. This protects each party against arbitrary changes in or cancellation of the contract. A consultant who signed a fund-raising contract with a summer repertory theater charged the theater one month's fee plus expenses when the contract was cancelled at the insistence of the artistic director, who had not been a party to the negotiations.

Some experts on consulting say that although contracts are sometimes unavoidable, as for example in government work, professional practice does not require them. The attitude of many professional consultants is that as long as the consultant does the work properly, follows the agreed plan, and gets results for the client, no formal contract is necessary. If the work proves unsatisfactory, a contract forcing continuance of the work would serve the interests of neither the client nor the consultant (Shay, 1981).

We believe with Shay that a letter of understanding is the most useful instrument of agreement. But it should be detailed and unambiguous and it should refer to and be accompanied by any written plans and descriptions of the problem that have preceded the agreement. The letter need not be legalistic, although an appropriate precaution would be to have it drafted or checked by an attorney.

155

Some experts prefer a formal contract because they anticipate the possibility of litigation should the client become dissatisfied with the outcome of the project. (This same line of thinking
has led many consultants to incorporate as a means of protecting
themselves against personal suits.) Certainly, the weaker the
document, the more it serves the interests of the consultant over
those of the client.

FACILITATING THE WORK

After you and your consultant have reached agreement on the
details of the assignment, the actual work begins. If you leave the
consultant entirely alone, you can be almost sure the work will
take longer and cost more than you planned. It may also be done
less to your satisfaction than if you had participated. You should
participate. You are the boss and without interfering with the
actual work, you should meet frequently with the consultant and
discuss progress and problems.

We repeat: working with a consultant is the same as working
with an employee—management never stops. Of course, the
more you trust the competence of an employee, the less you have
to supervise— but only up to a point.

You may wonder how you can help the consultant, especially
since the consultant is there to help you. The answer is the same.
You manage, and you facilitate. That is your job. You can facilitate by making the consultant feel part of your team and by
making certain that your management team cooperates with the
consultant in the assignment. You can make the consultant
comfortable in office space where he or she can spread out, think
in solitude, and interview employees in private. The privacy will
make interviews more productive and therefore more valuable in
the subsequent analysis. Such arrangements will alleviate disruption of normal work patterns and will save the consultant's
time in travelling back and forth to his or her own office.

Free up employee time for interviews and, if necessary, approve overtime pay. Assign clerical staff to help with the paper-
work. Direct executives to assist the consultant in gathering and
analyzing information. This latter task will not only expedite the

156

consultant's work; it will also give the assigned executives experience, insight, and knowledge about the problem the consultant is working to solve. Bear in mind our earlier point that the greatest benefit a company can gain from a consultant is the transfer of expert knowledge and skills to company employees.

Company people can help in other ways. Salespeople can gather information from customers. Staff specialists in law, real estate, and production technology can make it unnecessary for the consultant to call in his own more expensive experts. Data processing and graphic arts departments can provide valuable services. Every possible use of company personnel and resources saves money.

You can also help by avoiding any company-induced delay in the consultant's starting time. The consultant schedules his time and staff for the engagement. You should respect that schedule; in so doing, you preserve your right to require the consultant to keep to the agreed schedule. Further, if there is a delay at the start of the engagement, the consultant's future commitments to other clients could interfere with his ability to complete your job on time.

When the time comes to begin the project, introduce the consultant and his team to your employees. If you are the company president, this introduction will serve to validate the work of the consultant and ensure that your people cooperate. If you are a middle-management executive, begin by introducing the consultant to your superiors. This gesture will show the consultant that he has the support of senior management.

In memos and meetings, explain to your employees and colleagues the consultant's assignment and the methods he or she will use. Such communication will encourage cooperation and relieve the inevitable anxieties that arise when an outsider comes poking around the shop. The main concern employees have about management consultants is that their jobs will be eliminated in a reorganization or that their responsibilities will be reduced or that they will be forced to undergo new training to hold their jobs.

Supervisors worry that consultants will interfere with work routines and schedules, either during the engagement or as a result of a new plan of organization. Reassure them, if you can,

without misleading them. Arrange interview schedules to minimize disruption. Take as few people as possible away from their
daily routine. Explain goals and methods.

A crucial benefit of such explanations is that they make clear
to everyone concerned why and how the work of the consultant
will help them. The explanations activate the self-interest and
cooperation of the supervisors. This approach provides supervisors with reasons to allow their people to take time out to work on
the project or to be interviewed.

Explanations also help ensure that no one will withhold
information. To work effectively, the consultant must be able to
obtain a full and willing sharing of information, including information that you and your executives may prefer to keep confidential.

Protection of turf is a powerful motive in withholding information. If you are determined to get a full and objective report
from the consultant, and thus the greatest possible value from
his services, you can become a valuable ally in breaking the turf
barrier to vital information. In doing so, be sure to make clear to
everyone that the consultant will respect people's confidences.
He is no invader, but a guest and helper, and his goal is to
enhance all turfs.

When you talk to the consultant, do not be afraid to reveal
your ignorance of his specialty. Never feign understanding. Ask
questions, and you will learn what you need to know about the
consultant's techniques and approach. The consultant may actually learn from the nature of your ignorance something important about the nature of the problem. Bear in mind the old saw
that ignorance is curable, but if left unattended, can be the cause
of serious problems. The consultant is an expert in the area of
your problem, and his expertise can serve not only to solve the
problem at hand, but also to cure your ignorance so that the same
problem does not arise again for you.

Give yourself as many opportunities as possible to learn from
the consultant and to share information with him. To this end,
schedule frequent meetings with the consultant to discuss the
problem and progress toward a solution. Most consultants will
respond cooperatively to your interest. Consultants like Henry
Ekstein (see Chapter 2) take the initiative in encouraging such

interaction as a crucial part of the consulting process. They draw information, insights, and solutions from their clients' people, and they leave their clients with a sense of participation in the problem-solving process. As a result, their clients are more committed to making recommended solutions work.

Do not hesitate to give the consultant feedback. If you are impressed with his progress or style, say so. Your comments will encourage him to work with interest and enthusiasm. If, on the other hand, you find that, for example, the consultant is browbeating in interviews, taking too long to complete investigations in the marketing department, or employing sloppy technique, you should say so.

MAINTAINING CONTROL

As Antony Jay (1977) observes, "You absolutely must stay in firm control of your professional so that you always know what he is doing, why, when it will be done, what its implications for, and repercussions on, the rest of the organization will be, and how much it is going to cost." Bear in mind that "firm control" does not only mean knowing what is going on. It also means guiding the consultant as appropriate, depending on your sense of what is required in the situation.

You should never let the consultant work without supervision. Nor should you delegate to the consultant your own responsibilities. The consultant is there to study and recommend, not to make decisions or give orders. Permitting the consultant to violate the proper role of a consultant weakens your position and compromises the ability of the consultant to do the job for which he was hired.

The only exceptions appear when the consultant is hired to train employees, install equipment, or set up and temporarily operate a new program. Of course, when company employees are assigned to the consultant as staff assistants, he is for the time being their supervisor.

The best way to stay in control of your consultant is through frequent meetings. These meetings can be used to discuss the problem being worked on, to exchange data, to share insights and ideas, and to review progress. These meetings will help you to keep track of changes in the situation and difficulties in the project and to hear from the consultant about balky interviews and obstructive executives. You can tell when the desired results begin to prove reasonable or unattainable. You can, as necessary, shift the consultant's efforts or redefine the project's goals. You can use the meetings to guide the consultant, prod your people, and otherwise keep the project on track.

A formal version of the meeting technique of supervision is the written progress report. A long-term project would ordinarily combine the two, with weekly meetings and monthly or quarterly progress reports. The progress report should briefly describe the project, describe what work has been accomplished, indicate what work still is to be done, note any changes in plans and obstacles that may require adjustments to the plan, and, finally, compare actual progress to the original schedule and budget. The progress report should also serve as an occasion for the consultant to bill the client for time and expenses to date.

Should you trust what the consultant says in meetings and progress reports? Yes and no. You should always place trust in your consultant as the basis of your working relationship. But you should never take anything for granted. Firsthand checks on actual work in progress are no sign of a lack of trust; they are the responsible action of any conscientious manager. The guideline is: "Tell me what's going on, and then *show* me what's going on."

Peterson and Kerin (1980) report that both buyers and suppliers of marketing research think that it is wise for buyers to conduct independent checks of suppliers' marketing data. Such checks have the effect of reenforcing trust and of keeping the suppliers honest.

When it comes time for the consultant to write the final report, you should take time to go over the proposed contents. Ideally, every word of the final report will have been anticipated in previous progress reports, meetings, and informal discussions. Nevertheless, you should be concerned at this crucial stage that the analyses contained in the report remain apt and the conclusions and recommendations are complete, timely, and of practical application. You have no use for recommendations which cannot be implemented by your business.

160

Usually, delivery of a consultant's final report waits upon an oral presentation to the top management of your company. At this stage, all the important questions should have been resolved, but the presentation to your top management still provides one last chance for any necessary clarification and an opportunity to check that the report covers every point in the original or revised job description. Should your top management raise legitimate questions about the final report, appropriate adjustments should be made even if the consultant is required to do additional thinking and research.

Reputable consultants will make such adjustments, although experience indicates that shortcomings in final reports usually reflect the constraining realities of the client business, not incompetence of the consultant. Shortcomings may reflect an inadequate definition of the problem or a need to resolve related problems that were not included in the project. In such cases, the consultant will have noted the constraints and inadequacies at the point they appeared prior to or during the project.

Such constraints and inadequacies may mean that an optimal solution to the central problem of the current project is impossible. They thus often lead to recommendations in the consultant's final report of further work to deal with them. A proposal by the consultant to do further work is an opportunity for you to evaluate the advantages of a long-term relationship with the consultant. If the consultant proposes further work, it is an indication that he or she is interested in the company and willing to work toward further improvement. There are consultants who propose further work as a source of steady income with little or no genuine interest in the client. The more closely you have worked with your consultant during the current project, the better able you will be to judge whether a continued engagement is necessary and whether the consultant is one you would invite back.

Some business people find it useful, after the final report has been submitted, to ask the consultant for a follow-up report commenting on how the consultant and the client worked together. In such a report, the focus is on personalities, control procedures, cooperation, and information sharing. The aim is to learn what was useful and what should be avoided in a future

161

engagement. The report may say nothing that the client and consultant do not already know, but it commits the evaluation to paper for future reference. Copies of this report should be kept by both the client and the consultant.

FOLLOWING THROUGH

Once the final report has been submitted, the consultant's responsibility ends. It is then time for you to follow through with implementation of the report's recommendations. You take from the report what you find valuable and applicable and ignore the rest. You have no obligation to use the recommendations in the report, but you do owe it to your company to weigh the results and reject recommendations only after careful evaluation and consideration of alternatives. You should depart from the plan of the report only for good reasons, such as changes in personnel or unforeseen changes in the situation. Otherwise the time, money, and effort spent on the project are wasted.

Unfortunately, a great many consultants' reports never leave the boardroom display shelf. Action is blocked by corporate inertia or adverse vested interests. People are unwilling to change their habits and behavior even when the need is plain and the recommended steps toward change are thoroughly documented and demonstrated. Resistance can mean (1) refusal to use a computer screen instead of paper, (2) adding new product lines, (3) shifting money from stockholder allocations to new equipment.

This is the main reason why a prerequisite to engaging a consultant is commitment by the company and all its key executives to making whatever changes the project finds necessary to solve a problem. Lacking such a commitment, changes, however persuasively documented, may never be made and the project to bring about change may be doomed to failure.

Many experienced consultants try to include in their plan of implementation a follow-up visit to the client several months after submission of the final report. The visit allows the consultant to check on whether recommendations are actually being implemented and on how well they are working. If the consultant finds inertia and inaction, he or she can attempt to stimulate action, correct any misunderstandings, and perhaps work in fresh ideas and new techniques. The usefulness of a built-in follow-up visit by the consultant cannot be underestimated. It may be essential to progress in solving the problem the project was designed to address.

Many projects end with recommendations that are fairly easy to implement. For example, one of Henry Ekstein's first consulting engagements was to find a way to save money on barge maintenance. The client company had 100 barges, each of which was out of action for 102 days every time it had to be scraped, derusted, and painted with four coats of paint. Ekstein recommended using four different colors of paint, so that the owners could tell when all but the last coat had worn away. They could then drydock the barge and scrape it without having to deal with rust. The barge would be out of service for only 36 days, and it would last longer as well.

Other projects produce recommendations that are much harder to implement. They may involve reorganizing a department or an entire company, building a permanent training program, replacing people, diversifying, merging, or acquiring or dropping product lines. In each case, there can be both human and technical complications. It may often pay to retain the consultant in situations where implementation is politically difficult, technically complicated, or requires delicate negotiation. The consultant has the advantage of experience, having managed similar changes before, and of familiarity with the problem and the planned solution. As an independent outsider, the consultant is not trapped in the inevitable network of power relationships that obstruct change by insiders. The consultant can act decisively and effectively under two conditions: if top management wants the change, and if the consultant has established trust among the employees in his objectivity.

Remember: following through means using the consultant's recommendations. That use can be positive—doing what the consultant recommends. It can also be negative—doing something different *after* careful evaluation of the recommendations or even after partial implementation. The one thing following through does *not* mean is ignoring the consultant's work

163

completely. Fat reports can be impressive, but ignored reports are a waste of money and time.

CLIENTS VERSUS CONSULTANTS

Two studies have compared the views of clients and consultants on what makes the consulting relationship work. They found several points of agreement and some interesting differences, apparently related to the attitudes of clients and consultants toward each other. Peterson and Kerin (1980) report on these points of agreement between marketing research clients and consultants:

1. Clients should have a clear understanding of their problem before contacting a consultant.
2. Clients should get consultants involved at an early stage.
3. Clients should investigate consultants' past clients, prior experience, and familiarity with the industry.
4. Clients should know what procedures and techniques their consultants will use.
5. Clients should check their consultant's data.
6. Clients should know precisely who will be doing the consulting work.

Clients are insistent that research proposals should always be obtained in writing. Consultants believe that clients should be willing to rely on the consultant's experience and expertise, and that clients should not choose their consultants solely on the basis of cost.

These differences suggest that clients do not always trust their consultants to do everything they promise, and that consultants resent not being trusted. Disreputable, untrustworthy consultants are out there doing business. Their presence in the industry justifies a cautious approach to the content of understandings with consultants.

Another reason for the cautious approach is that misunderstandings can occur between perfectly honest people. We recommend that clients always put agreements with consultants into writing. We recommend that clients always run a thorough professional check on the prospective consultant's background and experience. We recommend that the client always check the consultant's data and results (and be suspicious of the consultant who balks at the check). We strongly recommend that the client keep a watchful eye on costs through the project.

On the other hand—and this is where the good judgment of the client must come into play—results can be far more important than the cost; the consultant *should* know more than the client; and trust is possible once the client and the consultant have established a close and lasting relationship.

John W. Zimmerman and Peter Tobia (1978) studied the opinions of clients and training consultants on what factors contribute to success or failure of a consulting engagement. Both clients and consultants agreed that important success factors are:

1. Agreement on clear, specific, visible objectives.
2. Agreement on evaluation methods.
3. Flexibility in approach.
4. Commitment to change.
5. Thorough consultant preparation.

Clients and consultants displayed notable differences in their opinions of what and who are usually responsible for poor results. Clients blamed themselves only for insufficient follow-up. Consultants blamed themselves for insufficient follow-up and for too little involvement of upper-level members of the consulting firm. Clients blamed consultants for using prepackaged programs and for failure to understand the client business. Consultants blamed clients for inadequate program structure, failure to gain the commitment of top management, and lack of openness.

If you have read this far, none of the above observations will have surprised you. Many factors contribute to a successful consulting engagement. If any one of them is missing, the chances of success are reduced. What is critical to the success of a consulting engagement is that both client and consultant accept responsibility for making sure that all the necessary factors are present and operational. It may be that only one party is to blame for shortcomings, but it is futile to spend time and energy nailing down that blame.

It is much more to the point for both consultant and client to encourage clarity, commitment, openness, understanding, follow-up, involvement, and other necessary virtues. Clients and consultants who follow this prescription conspire to create a climate for success. Consultants emerge from successful engagements with enhanced reputations and clients emerge with healthier, wealthier businesses.

Appendix:

Members of the
Association of Managment
Consulting Firms (ACME, Inc.)

It is impossible to list all available consultants, however much we might like to do so. There are, you may recall, over 70,000 of them. However, we can list a number of the major consulting firms. We have chosen to list those firms that belong to ACME, Inc., along with the locations of their branch offices, as given in ACME's membership directory. If you wish to engage a consultant, you may be tempted to go no further than this list, stopping in your search as soon as you have found one or two possibilities in your state or city. You will do better for yourself if you check with ACME to find consultants whose specialties fit your needs. You might also check with some of the consultant's groups we list in Chapter 8. *Do not* pick consultants blindly.

ACME MEMBERS   **BRANCH OFFICES**

Alexander & Alexander, Inc.
    16 Wilton Road
    Westport, CT 06880
    203-226-0404

ACME Members cont'd

Archer, Smith & Associates s.a.   Greece, Saudi Arabia
   6, Place Albert Leemans
   B-1050 Brussels, Belgium
   (02) 538-5999 Telex 24540 ASA

George S. Armstrong & Co., Inc.
   2 Park Avenue
   New York, NY 10016
   212-889-2280

The Austin Company
   Management Consulting Division
   820 Davis Street
   Evanston, IL 60201
   312-869-3130

Ayers, Whitmore & Company, Inc.
   Park Avenue Plaza
   55 East 52nd Street
   New York, NY 10055
   212-909-5700

Theodore Barry & Associates   NY, GA, IL, DC
   1520 Wilshire Boulevard
   Los Angeles, CA 90017
   213-413-6080

Bavier, Bulger & Goodyear, Inc.
   270 Amity Road
   New Haven, CT 06525
   203-389-1534

Roland Berger & Partner GMBH   Dusseldorf & Hannover,
   Germany
   Truderinger Strasse 13   Italy, France,
   England, Brazil
   8000 Munchen 80   Japan, South Africa
   (089) 41 76–1 Telex 522761

Betterley Consulting Group   TX, CA
   One Newton Executive Park
   Newton, MA 02162
   617-965-8420

The Billings Group
    One Main Street
    Concord, MA 01742
    617-369-2790

Case and Company, Inc.   CT, IL, CA
    90 Park Avenue
    New York, NY 10016
    212-687-9010

CH2M Hill Management   GA, OR, CO, WA
Consulting Division
    2200 Powell Street
    Emeryville, CA 94608
    415-652-2426

Cresap, McCormick and Paget   DC, IL, CA, GA
    245 Park Avenue   England, Australia
    New York, NY 10167
    212-953-7000

Herbert W. Davis and Company
    111 Charlotte Place
    Englewood Clifs, NJ 07632
    201-871-1760

Decision Sciences Corporation   NY
    528 Fox Pavilion
    Jenkintown, PA 19046
    215-887-1970

Drake Sheahan/Stewart Dougall, Inc .IL
    P.O. Box 1918
    New York, NY 10156
    212-689-8666

The Emerson Consultants, Inc.
    30 Rockefeller Plaza
    New York, NY 10112
    212-245-5738

Bertrand Frank Associates, Inc.
    475 Fifth Avenue
    New York, NY 10017
    212-685-4460

169

ACME Members cont'd

Walter Frederick Friedman & Co., Inc.
111 Northfield Avenue
West Orange, NJ 07052
201-325-3700
Garr Industries, Inc.
1240-50 Powers Ferry Road
Marietta, GA 30067
404-955-6142
Gottfried Consultants, Inc.   Lafayette, CA
3435 Wilshire Boulevard
Los Angeles, CA 90010
213-387-2271
Group Arcon
800 Wilshire Boulevard
Los Angeles, CA 90017
213-680-4550
A. S. Hansen, Inc.   GA, TX, CO, CA, TN,
1080 Green Bay Road   WI, LA, NY, FL, OK,
Lake Bluff, IL 60044   DC, KS
312-234-3400
The Hay Group   GA, MA, IL, OH, TX,
229 South 18th Street   MO, CA, MN, NY, WA,
Rittenhouse Square   CA, MN, NY, WA,
Philadelphia, PA 19103   DC, Mexico, Brazil, etc.
215-875-2300
Hayes/Hill Incorporated   NY, TX, South Africa
312 West Randolph
Chicago, IL 60606
312-984-5250
Hickling-Johnston Limited
415 Yonge Street, 10th Floor
Toronto, Canada M5B 2E7
416-977-2811
Daniel D Howard Associates, Inc.
307 North Michigan Avenue
Chicago, IL 60601
312-372-7041

170

Ingersoll Engineers Incorporated
707 Fulton Avenue
Rockford, IL 61103
815-987-6110

JMA Consultants, Inc.
3-1-22 Shiba Park
Minato-ku, Tokyo 105, Japan
(03) 434-7331

J. Lloyd Johnson Associates, Inc.
778 Frontage Road
Northfield, IL 60093
312-441-7060

A. T. Kearney, Inc.   VA, GA, MA, OH, TX,
222 South Riverside Plaza   CO, CA, NY,
Chicago, IL 60606   Netherlands, Belgium
312-648-0111

Kensington Management Consultants, Inc.
25 Third Street
Stamford, CT 06905
203-327-9860

Klein & Saks, Inc.
1001 Connecticut Avenue, N.W.
Washington, DC 20036
202-331-1227

Lester B. Knight & Associates, Inc.   DC, CA, NY
549 West Randolph Street
Chicago, IL 60606
312-346-2100

Krall Management Incorporated
Valley Forge Plaza
King of Prussia, PA 19406
215-337-8444

LWFW, Inc. Group
12700 Park Central, Suite 1805
Dallas, TX 75251
214-650-0503

171

ACME Members cont'd

Management Campus, Inc.
2000 Clearview Avenue, Suite 92
Atlanta, GA 30340
404-458-9021

H. B. Maynard and Company, Inc.   NC, IL, CT, CA, NJ, DC
235 Alpha Drive
Pittsburgh, PA 15238
412-963-8l00

McCormick & Company   AZ, IL
303 South Broadway
Tarrytown, NY 10591
914-631-7100

Paul B. Mulligan & Co., Inc.
Franklin Office Center
2 Skiff Street
Hamden, CT 06514
203-248-5881

Naremco Services, Inc.
60 East 42nd Street
New York, NY 10165
212-697-0290

Nolan, Norton & Company   IL, England
One Forbes Road
Lexington, MA 02173
617-862-8820

Norris & Elliott, Inc.
85 East Gay Street
Columbus, OH 43215
614-221-1514

ORU Group, Inc.   TX
111 West 40th Street
New York, NY 10018
212-730-1286

Albert Ramond & Associates, Inc.   Chicago, IL
   5005 Newport Drive
   Rolling Meadows, IL 60008
   312-577-6868

Rath & Strong, Inc.   CA
   21 Worthen Road
   Lexington, MA 02173
   617-861-1700

Risk Planning Group, Inc.
   722 Post Road
   Darien, CT 06820
   203-655-9791

Runzheimer and Company, Inc.   IL
   Runzheimer Park
   Rochester, WI 53167
   414-534-3121

Kurt Salmon Associates, Inc.   GA, TX, NC, CA,
   350 Fifth Avenue   TN, NJ
   New York, NY 10118
   212-564-3690

Sibson & Company, Inc.   NY, CA, IL
   777 Alexander Road
   Princeton, NJ 08540
   609-452-8500

The Sims Consulting Group, Inc.
   919 East Fair Avenue
   P.O. Box 646
   Lancaster, OH 43130
   614-654-1091

Summerour & Associates, Inc.   SC, NY, Hong Kong,
   Peachtree Center   Montreal
   241 Peachtree Street, N.E.
   Atlanta, GA 30303
   404-577-4632

ACME Members cont'd

Temple, Barker & Sloane, Inc.
33 Hayden Avenue
Lexington, MA 02173
617-861-7580

Towers, Perrin, Forster & Crosby   GA, MA, IL, OH, TX,
600 Third Avenue   MI, CA, WI, MN, PA,
New York, NY 10016   MO, WA, CT, FL, DC,
212-309-3400   Australia, Europe,
                                    Canada, etc.

Transportation and Distribution   NY
Associates, Inc.
1818 Market Street
Philadelphia, PA 19103
215-299-8080

K. W. Tunnell Company, Inc.   IL
Valley Forge Plaza
1150 First Avenue
King of Prussia, PA 19406
215-337-0820

Robert M. Wald and Associates, Inc.
45 Mercantile Place
Pasadena, CA 91105
213-792-7111

Emanuel Weintraub Associates, Inc.
Polygon Plaza
2050 Center Avenue
Fort Lee, NJ 07024
201-947-2404/201-489-7920

Welling & Woodard, Inc.   CA
16 Bruce Park Avenue
P.O. Box 1037
Greenwich, CT 06830
203-622-0230

174

Werner Associates, Inc.
   111 West 40th Street
   New York, NY 10018
   212-730-1280

Belgium

John P. Young & Associates
   (Aust.) Pty, Ltd.
   2 Fordholm Road
   Hawthorn, Vic. Australia 3122
   03/819 1185

Sidney, Newcastle
Brisbane, Wayville,
West Perth; Wellington,
NZ

BIBLIOGRAPHY

Brown, Stephen W., and Donald W. Jackson, Jr., "On choosing a management consultant," *Arizona Business,* October 1975, pp. 9–14.

Dexter, Albert S., and Bernhard J. Schwab,"Making your call on a consultant a success," *The Business Quarterly,* Autumn 1975, pp. 79–86.

Drucker, Peter F., "Our entrepreneurial economy," *Harvard Business Review,* January–February 1984, pp. 59–64.

Fox, Harold W., "Quasi-boards: Useful small business confidants,"*Harvard Business Review,* January–February 1982, pp. 158–165.

Frankenhuis, Jean Pierre, "How to get a good consultant," *Harvard Business Review,* November–December 1977, pp. 133–139.

Fuchs, Jerome H., *Making the Most of Management Consulting Services* (New York: AMACOM, 1975).

Fuchs, Jerome H., "Management consulting services reduce costs," *The Office,* January 1978, pp. 130–132.

Golde, Roger A., "Breaking the barriers to small business planning," Small Business Administration pamphlet "Management Aids for Small Manufacturers" No. 179.

Greiner, Larry E., and Robert O. Metzger, *Consulting to Management* (Englewood Cliffs, NJ: Prentice-Hall, 1983).

Hunt, Alfred, *The Management Consultant* (New York: Ronald Press, 1977).

Interview with Alan Kennedy, April 1984, *Inc.*, pp. 108–117.

Jay, Antony, "Rate yourself as a client," *Harvard Business Review*, July–August 1977, pp. 84–92.

Kahn, Joseph P., "A good word about consultants," *Inc.*, January 1984, pp. 57–60.

Kelley, Robert E., "Should you have an internal consultant?" *Harvard Business Review*, November–December 1979, pp. 110–120.

Lawson, James C., "Are computer consultants necessary?" *Wall Street Computer Review*, July 1984, pp. 50–54.

Lee, David A., "Guidelines for the selection of a consultant," *American Laboratory*, June 1983, pp. 89–91.

Levinson, Harry, "Conflicts that plague family businesses," *Harvard Business Review*, March–April 1971, pp. 90–98.

Mahoney, Richard J., "What to do after the consultants go home," *Business Week*, February 13, 1984, p. 17.

Mamis, Robert A., "Sparring partners," *Inc.*, March 1984, pp. 43–50.

PATCA, *Annual Survey of Consulting Rates and Business Practices* (PATCA, 1983–1984).

Peterson, Robert A., and Roger A. Kerin, "The effective use of marketing research consultants," *Industrial Marketing Management, 9* (1980), pp. 69–73.

Schein, Edgar H., *Process Consultation: Its Role in Organizational Development* (Reading, MA: Addison–Wesley, 1969).

Shay, Philip W., *How to Get the Best Results from Management Consultants* (New York: ACME, Inc., 1974, 1981).

Shenson, Howard L., *How to Strategically Negotiate the Consulting Contract* (Woodland Hills, CA: H. L. Shenson).

Shenson, Howard L., *How to Select, Manage, and Compensate Consultants, Trainers, and Professional Practitioners* (Woodland Hills, CA: H. L. Shenson, 1980).

Thurston, Philip H., "Should smaller companies make formal plans?" *Harvard Business Review,* September–October 1983, pp. 162–188.

Turner, Arthur N., "Consulting is more than giving advice," *Harvard Business Review,* September–October 1982, pp. 120–129.

von Hippel, Eric, "Get new products from customers," *Harvard Business Review,* March–April 1982, pp. 117–122.

Zimmerman, John W., and Peter M. Tobia, "Programming your outside consultants for success," *Training and Development Journal,* December 1978, pp. 14–19.

Index

181

▣ Probus Publishing Company Presents

Titles in Investment/ Personal Finance

The Investor's Equation: Creating Wealth Through Undervalued Stocks, by William M. Bowen IV and Frank P. Ganucheau III. ISBN 0-917253-00-0.

Stock Index Options: Powerful New Tools for Investing, Hedging, and Speculating, by Donald T. Mesler. ISBN 0-917253-02-7.

Winning the Interest Rate Game: A Guide to Debt Options, by Frank J. Fabozzi. ISBN 0-917253-01-9.

Low Risk Strategies for the High Performance Investor, by Thomas C. Noddings. ISBN 0-917253-09-4.

Maximize Your Gains: Tax Strategies for Today's Investor, by Robert W. Richards. ISBN 0-917253-10-8.

Increasing Your Wealth in Good Times and Bad, by Eugene M. Lerner and Richard M. Koff. ISBN 0-917253-06-X.

The Insider's Edge: Maximizing Investment Profits Through Managed Futures Accounts, by Bertram Schuster and Howard Abell. ISBN 0-917253-12-4.

The Handbook of Mortgage-Backed Securities, Frank J. Fabozzi, editor. ISBN 0-917253-04-3.

Personal Economics: A Guide to Financial Health and Well-Being, by Robert A. Kennedy and Timothy J. Watts. ISBN 0-917253-08-6.

Titles in Business

Revitalizing Your Business: Five Steps to Successfully Turning Around Your Company, by Edmund P. Freiermuth. ISBN 0-917253-05-1.

Compensating Yourself: Personal Income, Benefits and Tax Strategies for Business Owners, by Gerald I. Kalish. ISBN 0-917253-07-8.

Getting Your Banker to "Yes": Tactics for the Entrepreneur, by Adam E. Robins. ISBN 0-917253-11-6.

For further information, call Probus Publishing Company at (312) 346-7985.